Transformative Conversations: The Heart of the Leadership Journey

Ada Gonzalez, Ph.D., LMFT

Transformative Conversations: The Heart of the Leadership Journey
ISBN-13: 978-0692401484
Copyright © 2015 by Ada Gonzalez, Ph.D., LMFT

Published by Logos Noesis
Typeset by Joshua Wong
Cover by Kevin Garcia, www.kgcreative.com
Printed in the United States of America. All rights reserved under International
Copyright Law.

Contents

Introduction: The Power of Dialogue

IF YOU'RE LIKE most leaders, you spend the majority of your day communicating. There's an endless stream of emails, meetings, hallway chats, phone calls, texts, Tweets, and Facebook messages. Perhaps you leave the office with a tired jaw and raw fingertips. If all of that communicating leaves you tired and with an empty feeling, you're not alone. Electronic discussions tend to be even more daunting, circular, and frustrating than face-to-face ones. Yet, part of your negative feelings could be ascribed to lack of real conversation in its highest form: dialogue.

In today's frenzied global economy, the challenges and decisions you face require more collaboration than ever before. Dialogue engages the often-forgotten power of conversation for helping organizations collaborate and innovate. As the 21st century progresses, the importance of mastering dialogue will be recognized as the heart of leadership.

In the following pages you will be introduced to the power of conversation. The purpose of this work is to encourage you to find ways to engage more effectively in face-to-face conversation. Dialogue is an often-overlooked pathway to success. It's rarely seen as an integral part of leadership.

Maybe you've grown so accustomed to having superficial conversations – always ready with an answer – that you rarely pause to reflect or ask questions that could move you toward deeper understanding. Perhaps you don't have the patience to deliberately slow down conversations so new understanding and meaning can emerge. It's possible you have forgotten that making meaning is the cradle of concerted action.

Many people confuse discussion for dialogue. They miss profound opportunities to share, listen, connect, reflect, and make meaning together. Effective communication isn't about sharing company policy and giving your team information. It isn't about presenting facts, profit columns, and projections. Nor is it about promoting approved answers and telling others things that will make them – and you – feel good.

Dialogue is a powerful practice. It's a special kind of conversation that permits and invites change. It's impossible to engage in it and come out the same. Effective dialogue transforms because it creates deeper understanding and meaning. This discovery process allows for new ways of seeing the world and making sense of it. It can lead to high-quality collective thinking and unprecedented transformation for you, your colleagues, and the company.

My love affair with dialogue started some decades ago when I began college in the United States. Since I was born in Cuba and spoke only Spanish, I had to start the process of mastering the English language. Suddenly, I was aware of each word's meaning and importance. Cuba brought constant censorship and fear, now I could freely explore words and marvel at their transformative powers. My relocation was freeing in countless ways, yet despite the shift from a communist to a democratic country, I still felt stifled at times. I longed for freedom of speech in Cuba; I longed for business leaders to wisely use their freedom of speech when I began consulting in America.

That's why I dedicated my career to helping people express their thoughts and feelings without being penalized. After 25 years of experience, I'm still perplexed by leaders who dismiss opportunities to become dialogue masters.

This book offers insight into how you can inspire, persuade, and connect. It shows how leading through transformative conversations can help you build trust and effectively guide change. It suggests practical approaches for gaining and using the collective wisdom that emerges from dialogue. You will learn how to blend humility and confidence to transform yourself and your organization by improving your dialogue skills.

Part I establishes the foundation. It addresses the need for dialogue and explains how leaders can create interactive conversations that matter.

Part II addresses basic practical guidelines that make transformative conversations possible. It explains the fundamental skills for effective dialogue. This section is highly practical and includes suggestions for becoming more skilled at using the building blocks of effective conversation.

At the end, we circle back to reiterate the important role dialogue plays in the leadership journey. This powerful core business element can lead to transformation and innovation.

We learn to speak in infancy. That doesn't mean you know how to communicate effectively. Investing the time to learn effective techniques for dialogue is like polishing your shoes. People will notice. You will stand taller. Let's get started!

Part I

Leading Through Transformative Conversations

Leading Through Transformative Conversations

Picture it. A meeting room in the School of Medicine. A new director. He's presenting to administrators, faculty, and staff for the first time. He's bursting with creative plans and innovative concepts. It's his time to shine. Go time. With careful execution, his detail-oriented plan will take the school from good to great. Maybe world class. He nails his PowerPoint. Ready to answer any and every question thrown at him, he invites comments. And then…deafening…crickets. Was that a yawn?

Puzzled at the lack of response and awkward silence his presentation generated, he paid me a visit. What was my take on his disheartening experience? He could not understand why his colleagues lacked enthusiasm and interest for what seemed like a common sense path to improvement. Wasn't it obvious to them? After all, he had the answers. They simply needed to get on board. Instead, they left him in an agonizing state of embarrassment. Paralyzed at the podium.

My assessment: he made one common – but critical – mistake. He got down to business before building the foundational connections needed to establish credibility and trust. He did not seek the expertise or involvement of the very individuals he wanted and needed to support his vision. They did not own the ideas. To them, his unfounded enthusiasm was a byproduct of his newbie status. "The new guy with the big, hairy audacious goal." They had seen similar pet projects come and go. Sounds good on paper; won't work in practical terms. They assumed the new director would quickly tire of waving his flag of change. Then everything would return to normal. Had the director established a personal connection with the others, a dialogue may have blossomed. Maybe it would have resulted in the positive changes he envisioned.

3

Many business leaders fall short – or fail miserably – when it comes to connecting and communicating effectively. They miss huge opportunities to earn the loyalty, trust, and confidence of their teams. It can cost them dearly. It doesn't have to.

Watson Wyatt's communication survey for 2009/2010 sums it up nicely. In essence, companies that project a voice of courage, innovation, and steadfastness are better at getting employee buy-in and hitting business objectives. On-target internal communications can keep employees focused on strategic goals, and even help retain those talented employees. Effective internal communication has a trickle-down effect too, as customers experience more consistent value. Shareholders reap the benefits of superior financial performance.

Why is this so important? The study showed that companies with effective communication strategies had a 47 percent higher total return to shareholders during a five-year period between 2004 and 2009. Imagine if that were your business. Imagine if polishing up your communication strategies and tactics could result in higher performance levels. Imagine if those efforts thrust you to the head of the pack, allowing your company to emerge from economic challenges before the competition. Wyatt showed in very practical terms that if someone, let's call her Carla Communicator, invested $100 in 2004 in a company with just so-so communication, she'd have $83 today. Had Carla invested her $100 in companies with highly effective communication practices, she'd have $130 in her wallet.

Bottom line. High-performing companies make communication a priority and use multiple resources to engage their employees in a dialogue. Employees receive information. Direction. A sense of belonging. The official company word plugs holes, keeping gossip, rumor, and speculation at bay.

Without effective communication, employees are left on their own to wonder. They fill their imaginations with fear, which leads to low morale and poor performance. Developing and executing a solid communication strategy takes work, no doubt. When you consider the alternative – 10 times the effort to correct misinformation – it makes good business sense to put your money where your mouth is, so to speak.

Now consider this. Competitive advantage appears to be linked to the social functioning of the workplace. The current climate requires employees to be flexible, resilient, and collaborative. They must possess a sense of self, and an awareness of others. This means that leaders of the new millennium must have the skills, confidence, and creativity to manage this dynamic social system: the workplace. Excellent communication is key. For people to work well together, they need to be able to communicate effectively.

Robert Kent, former dean of Harvard Business School said, "In business, communication is everything." He wasn't kidding. Top-level managers typically spend 75 to 80 percent of their time engaged in written or oral communication. At the highest ranks, 90 percent of the day is allocated to communication activities. Once considered a soft skill, communication savvy has earned increasing rank as one of the most critical leadership skills. Evidence continues to support its worth. Surprisingly, many leaders continue to dismiss its power. That's a big mistake.

Think about your life. Now consider the paths your family, friends, neighbors, and colleagues have chosen. You're all on a quest to make meaning. For some of you it's deliberate and strategic. Others arrive at it on a more passive and subconscious level. But it's there, in each of you. When faced with dramatic changes or events, do you have a shared need to make meaning together? How does it occur? In a word: dialogue. Private discussions. Public discourse. They constantly influence each other, taking your brains, hearts, and imaginations to places unknown. Dialogue is central to leadership. It's indispensable for leading change. It's key to personal and organizational growth.

Dialogue is the best way to foster collaboration and rediscover connections with others. It contributes to the success of spreading messages – both official and informal – through organizations. It's the glue that binds relationships and creates an environment of appreciation. It's within that environment that we can trade ideas with each other and venture into new territory. It takes practice to bring the invisible world of thought and feeling to expression. It's required to feel alive. To grow. To thrive.

Nurture transformative conversations, reap the benefits

There are many good reasons why it's important to lead through conversations. Here are a few of the most impactful. Think about your own organizational structure as you consider the following scenarios.

Poor communication is pricey

Is ineffective communication truly costly to a company? Is it ever.

A global study sponsored by Siemens Enterprise Communications, conducted by SIS International Research, tells the staggering story. On average, 70 percent of employee respondents of small and medium businesses with up to 400 employees said they spend 17.5 hours each week addressing the "pain points" caused by communication's barriers and failures.

In addition, researchers determined the time spent each week dealing with communication issues was more than 50 percent higher in companies with more than 20 workers. What's that mean for the bottom line? Companies of 100 employees could be losing more than $500,000 each year by not addressing their most painful communications issues. In order of estimated cost, the study identified five pain points:

1. Inefficient coordination
2. Waiting for information
3. Unwanted communications
4. Customer complaints
5. Barriers to collaboration

Your organization has likely suffered from one or more of these pain points. Take a moment to reflect on your team's performance. When your employees can't get their communications in sync, do they miss deadlines? How much time is wasted when Employee A needs information from Employee B, who can't be reached or won't respond? Is it because he's sifting through unwanted communications, like vendor voicemails and emails about the staff potluck? Now both employees are distracted, unproductive, and missing deadlines. How's their morale? Are they as disgruntled as the client on hold, waiting feverishly to tell a "real human being" about her dissatisfaction with your service standards? When your team finally agrees these issues need to be addressed, who can't make the meeting? Who would rather text under the table than address pressing issues?

This vicious cycle of ineffective communication can cost your company big bucks. Companies can lose thousands – millions – of dollars by not addressing communication issues. This doesn't even account for failed change efforts and conflicts that develop between leaders unskilled at nurturing transformative conversations. What's worse, these costs are hidden. Invisible on the spreadsheets. There isn't a line on the balance sheet that accounts for lousy communication. No red flag appears with a note indicating "lost productivity due to miserable meeting" or "missed business opportunity because response to customers sucked." The costs are real. They can be damaging. Devastating. However, they can be mitigated. You could save significant amounts of money by honing communication skills at every level. An investment in effective business communication practices will yield a significant return.

Changing environments require more sophisticated communication

Organizations are becoming increasingly flatter, as layers of management between the employee base and executives disappear. There is an increased emphasis on recruiting and retaining a diverse workforce. Work teams try to achieve greater productivity and profitability, as creative units blend their instincts and skills for the greater good. All of these factors have made communication imperative to organizational success. The days of barking orders and expecting results have gone the way of the typewriter. Goodbye autocratic leadership model. Hello collaborative leadership model. Effective communication is required.

How does your organization use teams? Whether they're functional, cross-functional, or self-directed, they all require communication. It is the primary element in building trust, promoting understanding, and influencing others. The collaboration that allows organizations to capitalize on the creative potential of a diverse workforce depends on communication. It is *the* way to transact business in this increasingly complex world.

Globalization demands effective communication

We are now in the age of the global economy. The competition is intense. The challenges can be countless. Businesses must find creative and innovative ways to navigate the competitive waters to improve success rates.

It's one of the toughest challenges as organizations attempt to engage in overseas commerce and evaluate global joint ventures. There are cultural nuances to consider in advertising campaigns. There are product adaptation requirements to research. All of it requires carefully crafted communication. When managed poorly, frustration and lost opportunities can result.

It's easy to see how the financial costs linked to ineffective communication can be high. It doesn't have to be that way. It circles back to investing in the communication skills of top and middle managers. This leads to increased productivity and decreased costs. The side effect is a positive environment where the stage is set for competing and succeeding in the changing global economy.

Leaders create interactive conversations

What qualities define a leader? Your brain might tick off leadership hallmarks like integrity, dedication, humility, assertiveness, and creativity. Central to all of that is a leader's ability to make conversations interactive and authentic. Poet and Fortune 500 consultant David Whyte said, "The core act of leadership must be the act of making conversations real."

Those instances of dialogue play out in human voices. As a leader, your voice is the public expression of your identity. The real deal. The unvarnished you. Who you are, where you came from, what you stand for. Above all, your voice is the expression of your authentic leadership.

Leadership is about creating opportunities for conversation. Talk may be cheap, but genuine dialogue is priceless. Your leadership voice shows itself in every conversation, interaction, and thought exchange, both verbal and written. It takes free-spirited conversation to generate smart ideas, influence others, and creatively solve problems. The quality of the conversations you facilitate shapes the quality of your interpersonal relationships, and ultimately, the organizational culture. It all happens through conversation.

As you polish your leadership skills, remember the power of transformative conversations. They drive change and enhance learning. Consciously nurture your conversations to:

- Build trust-based relationships.

- Create opportunities for new and more meaningful possibilities.
- Increase engagement, shared commitment, and accountability.
- Make connection and collaboration possible.

Leadership is an ongoing interactive conversation that pulls people into an energetic sphere where they're motivated to realize their potential. Through conversations, you can inspire, influence, connect, and mobilize people to take action and embrace change. Notice how many essential actions that business and political leaders engage in happen through conversations. As you begin to think in these terms, it becomes easier to see why leaders should consider conversations a powerful core business process.

1   Conversation Matters

EVENINGS ON THE PORCH. It seems so simple, but it's one of my fondest memories of childhood in Cuba. After dinner, it was common to melt into those squeaky rocking chairs. On our porch or on the neighbor's porch. It didn't matter where. What mattered was the conversation that swirled around those rockers. I loved listening in as my parents and friends shared stories, traded recipes, told tales, and gave advice. It was a free – and often entertaining – education in business, politics, religion, health, love, and life. I was hooked. My lifelong fascination with conversation was off and running.

Where's the buzz?

Fast-forward a few decades. As I began consulting with organizations, I could quickly get a feel for the enthusiasm of the workforce based on the buzz of conversations. I'd note the clusters of people discussing a project or trading information. The executive clique often hung together. Their topics ranged from financial solvency to family activities. Their exchanges connected them as living, breathing, feeling individuals, not just as company functionaries.

That's all changed. Today when I walk into a workspace I hear lifeless keyboards clicking. Silence. Human interactions are rare. Employees block out the world and their co-workers by inserting ear buds. It's common to see leaders email, text, or browse the Internet in the midst of conversation. It can be a dizzying and disheartening scene for someone who recalls the rich exchange and human interaction of those evenings on the porch. It's time to revive the lost art of conversation.

Is old-school chat over-rated?

Old-fashioned conversations are worth their weight in gold. The multi-dimensional nature of today's work requires more sophisticated and deliberate levels of communication than ever before. Though texting has its benefits, it leaves a lot to chance. Consider the social cues lost to texting. An emoticon or insertion of "LOL" can hardly replace the richness of face-to-face conversation or belly-busting laughter.

Misunderstandings are likely to occur in today's text-centric world. Opportunities for innovation can be lost. Teams quickly unravel when they miss or exclude key points. Interpersonal relations remain the foundation for building consensus. This requires leaders to be real-time conversational artists.

Imagine if companies invested as much in improving the frequency and substance of real-time conversations as they did in advancing technologies. Collaboration is required for leadership success. Yet it requires much of what technology as a communication vehicle cannot offer: awareness of social nuances and nonverbal cues. Smooth and effective relationships are best nurtured through conversation.

When you think about team building, do you shudder at the thought of a Kum Ba Yah exercise? Like the kind used to kick off conferences? A more effective approach to team building is using stories and conversations that center on real life, real people, and real issues. Most turning points – those pivotal moments when colleagues say "Aha!" – occur during conversations. Change goes hand in hand with conversation. It is in conversation that people influence and become influenced, present and seek new opportunities, and nurture and accept innovation. All key types of conversations have merit for leaders, but none so much as dialogue. It remains the most effective way to build the connections that foster collaboration and change.

Transformative conversations and connections

To illustrate the transformative power of conversations, allow me to describe the journey I led an impressive group of executives through during a recent retreat. It's early spring. We're secluded in a beautiful, calming conservation park. Comfortable facilities, a singing brook, a lodge.

The table is set for this busy group of executives to reflect, dialogue, and sharpen their team building skills. It's day one of three. Their restlessness is visible. They want to get down to business, yet they recognize the need for pause. They're mid-merger. New team members are on board. Meetings are less than cohesive. It's time to regroup.

Our intimate group gathers in a circle of comfy couches and chairs. In the middle, a low-profile table displays the following objects. They represent the basic elements required for successful conversations.

Candle: It lights the fires of passion that include dissent, suffering, and confusion, but also possibilities, transformation, and warmth.

Shell: It represents the calm, clear, soothing power of water, plus the power, danger, and energy required for change.

Wooden basket filled with chocolate: Symbolizing a nurturing container, it will bring safety, trust, and comfort to the group dialogue.

Talking stick: This underscores the importance of taking turns and following proper dialogue etiquette.

In addition, the executives have displayed their own symbolic contributions. What item represents each person's hopes for the retreat? There's super glue, a multi-use tool, Miracle Grow, and signs bearing words like "trust" and "respect." After working together for nearly two years, we've established trust within the group. They trust me. More importantly, they trust the process of dialogue and each other. This trust factor is paramount to the success of our retreat. We will share feelings, thoughts, dreams, and tough concerns. Trust is required.

As we eat and laugh together, the bonds strengthen. The participants are able to move past misunderstandings that previously stood in the way of integration. There is renewed energy for taking risks and responsibilities. They are excited to forge a new path for the company's future.

It's now day three, and they report a sense of accomplishment. By slowing the hurry of daily corporate life, they feel accomplished in a refreshing way. They feel at peace. They have less tension. Their headaches are gone. Within conversations, there are now comfortable silences rather than a flurry of follow-up comments. The process of thinking and sharing has slowed down and gone deeper. Now that they've reprogrammed themselves to reflect, connect, check meanings, gain understanding, and share from the heart, they are better positioned to make decisions. They are wiser leaders.

Their post-retreat comments provided even deeper insight into the magnitude of their learning. They felt their leadership team gained strength as a unit as they learned to arrive at decisions in a collaborative way. With their defenses down, they were able to discuss topics and ask questions openly. Perhaps most importantly, they took time to think before answering. Pausing gave them a chance to see the diversity of thought within the group as an ally, rather than a threat.

A week later I facilitated a meeting with the same leadership team, only this time the company's middle managers were included. It was exciting to witness the leadership team show off their improved communication skills. They kept a relaxed stance, listened more closely, asked genuine questions, and sought feedback. They said it was their most effective combined meeting ever.

So, what was different? Their deep dive into dialogue at the prior retreat contributed to the easy rapport and genuine interest they showed in the larger group setting. As a result, the executive team gained the trust and collaboration they craved from the middle managers. Bravo.

We live in a world where millions of media messages vie for our attention. The proverbial to-do list has grown to obscene proportions. Our consumer choices are exponential. It's easy to understand how we miss a lot in our quest to make sure we never miss anything. As a leader, it's critical to slow down, look inside, and understand yourself. It's equally important to savor beauty, nature, conversations, and those priceless heart connections. View time spent in dialogue as a valuable investment.

The roots of dialogue

Conversation is central to every dealing in every society. It sustains daily life. It propels life forward. It helps businesses meet their missions and teams win championships. It allows governments to take concerted action. Conversation is also the cornerstone for evaluating and launching improvement plans and innovations.

To learn about a specific society, simply look at the way they make meaning. How do they arrive at consensus? What are their values? How do they conceive and interpret the world? To answers these questions we have to analyze their conversations and understand how they communicate. Many ancient societies have influenced how the Western world makes sense of present reality. Here are a few examples:

Indigenous cultures and circles

Throughout the ages, indigenous cultures have practiced the art of dialogue by sitting in a circle and talking. History often refers to council circles, women's circles, elders' circles, and campfire circles. It's where stories were told and retold. Where meanings evolved. Whether in the Americas, Africa, Iceland, Ireland, Australia, the Pacific Islands or any other pocket of the globe, circles were the cradle of systems, civilizations, and organized society.

The ancients believed that a circle enclosed space, and from the perfect freedom of this emptiness the spirit joined the creative processes of life with the infinite universe. The spirit – the Creator – was the eternal parent giving birth to all things. When life processes were connected with the spirit and the fundamental principle of the circle was given birth, all things evolved to completion through the circle. All things were created within the circle.

The indigenous view of the circle further supports the concept. It has been expressed that an Indian does everything in circular fashion because the power of the universe works in circles. All things attempt to be round. The sky. The earth. All the stars. Even the wind, in its greatest power, whirls. Birds create circular nests. The seasons return to where they were. A man's life is circular, from childhood to childhood.

Within a circle, individuals build relationships and establish rapport before business is discussed. Much of the circle time may be spent establishing the foundation for the honest dialogue that will ensue. Participants use personal stories to access wisdom, as life experience is often regarded as more valuable and credible than advice. Stories of joy and pain, struggle and triumph, vulnerability and strength help unravel the issue at hand.

Because storytelling engages people on many levels – emotional, spiritual, physical, and mental – listeners absorb stories differently than they do advice. Discussing values, creating guidelines, and exposing personal details all create the foundation for dialogue. This build up engages participants' spirits, emotions, and intellect.

Christianity

According to the Judeo-Christian tradition, the world itself sprang forth as a result of a dialogue among the members of the Triune God (Genesis 1). It was the Word of God that converted God's plan into action (Genesis 1). Later, in the Gospel of John, Jesus is described as the Word incarnate, who is both God the Creator and God made flesh. By discarding his hierarchical robes and becoming the "light" that "shines in the darkness," Jesus initiates making God known through a dialogue that is "full of grace and truth" (John 1:1-18).

The Gospel of John, more than any other, presents Jesus in dialogue with individuals of all walks of life: men and women, Jews and Gentiles, rich and poor, uneducated fishermen and doctors of the law, sick and whole, believers and nonbelievers, criminals and soldiers. He taught through stories, metaphors, and questions. Jesus was a master at introducing openings for conversations to occur.

From Greece to Early America

The importance of dialogue can be seen through the lens of cultures far and wide. The Greeks saw dialogue as the cornerstone of civic practice, inseparable from self-governing. Their capacity for exchanging ideas among themselves established the foundation for democracy. Many present-day words and concepts about dialogue originated from the Greeks. One could argue that early American settlers' desire for freedom of expression emanated from ancient Greece.

The settlers' harrowing journey to the shores of the New World created a rich environment for dialogue, as they communicated about their most cherished beliefs, values, and traditions. Trust was central to their dialogue, as they wanted to share openly, without fear of being condemned as dangerous or criminal.

Upon their arrival, the American settlers survived and thrived by making meaning together. This included exploring the New World's possibilities, overcoming its challenges, and making better decisions as a unit than they could have as individuals. Sewing circles, correspondence committees, and tavern talks were the womb that nurtured and eventually gave birth to the American Revolution for Independence. Just as the ancient

Greeks used dialogue to create a democracy, the settlers made meaning together in conversation, which led to the birth of a nation.

Dialogue is as critical in the present world as it was for the ancient Greeks and early settlers. Dialogue is central to life. Being alive requires it. To live requires asking questions, responding, agreeing, disagreeing, and offering feedback and opinions. It's ironic then, that today's society seems to challenge its merit.

Is today's tendency to diminish conversation a challenge to society's ability to thrive without conversations, the essential glue that has always bound cultures? Renewal can only be achieved through dialogue. The Greeks needed it. The settlers needed it. Today's fragmented society certainly needs renewal through dialogue to keep the democratic principles alive and ensure forward movement.

Dissecting dialogue

The word "dialogue" comes from the Greek word *dialogos*. "Logos" means "the word" and "dia" means *through*. This combination suggests an image of a stream flowing among and through people. The stream carries meaning. From this a new understanding may emerge as shared meaning. In dialogue, there is a free flow of meaning that can be the catalyst for change.

In the most ancient meaning of the word, logos meant, "to gather together." This suggests intimate awareness, or a relationship. It's even hinted at in the first words of the Book of John in the Bible: "In the beginning was the Word." This might be interpreted as "In the beginning was the relationship." It could be said that in dialogue, people think together in relationship.

Think about the word "you." Jewish theologian M. Buber said, "Whoever says 'You' does not have something; he has nothing. But he stands in relation." To find the word between requires genuine contact. Contact of minds. Contact of hearts. Contact of shared humanity. That contact is critical for innovation to occur, as even the most powerful motivations can be wasted if people are not connected in the process of creating the future.

Webster's New Unabridged Dictionary offers another definition of dialogue: "An interchange and discussion of ideas, especially when open and frank, as in seeking mutual understanding or harmony." This definition goes far beyond the concept of a basic conversation. It suggests a solid, mutually respectful way of learning and testing knowledge.

What does an interactive dialogue mean in the context of organizations? Interacting, or performing reciprocal acts, has a goal of discovering the various meanings people assign to attributes, values, and objectives. By engaging in an interactive dialogue, people will arrive at a more robust list of options than would have resulted from an individual effort.

Dialogue requires participants to abandon certainty and increase awareness. People must open their minds to the possibilities that emerge from being in relationships with others. An individual's position is not final. The goal of dialogue isn't necessarily truth, but rather, meaning. Dialogue can be the vehicle for solving – and dissolving – problems. Think of dialogue as a meeting between two people, the process of talking *with* – not *to* – another person. It's an open-ended, dynamic, living experience of inquiry between people that results in greater understanding.

As a leader, you dialogue with countless individuals with the goal of achieving mutual understanding. It requires you to engage your entire being in an active listening relationship. This is a powerful way to rediscover and nurture connections with others. Does it feel different than normal conversation, debate, or discussion? It should.

As you commit yourself to speaking and listening more deliberately, you will gain deeper understanding. Your interpersonal relationships will improve as you create a safe environment. Others will begin to inquire freely, while openly sharing their thoughts and feelings. In the heat of challenging moments, you will discover new ways to learn and reflect.

Be open to the experience of looking for hidden meanings, assumptions, values, traps, voices, and the invisible forces of interactions. In dialogue, the possibilities for newness, meaning making, and understanding are limitless.

Dialogue is a journey of change

Human beings evolve. Organizations change. Dialogue provides the springboard for the transformation. It also functions to bind the mosaic that constitutes the composite of the self in one coherent whole. The stories we tell others and ourselves can permit or hinder the self-agency needed for change. From an interpretive perspective, change is part of dialogue. It's the sharing of stories through the ages, the knowledge of people, places and events acquired through conversation. At the same time, it's the varying interpretations assigned to past, present, and future occurrences. It contributes to the development of your future self.

Dialogue can change the meaning of personal and organizational experience, just as situations can acquire new possibilities and people can explore many truths. Dialogue allows individuals to overcome their fears, gain confidence, and release the creative energy required for new and innovative ideas to flow.

Transformative conversations flow not so much from individuals, but from the collective words of people in relationships. In today's complex business landscape, change is unlikely to occur via executive order. Some leaders mistakenly believe that if they design a solid change plan, employees will automatically implement it. That's rarely the case, as 65 to 85 percent of change efforts fail. Even with a solid design, a flawed implementation plan can spoil success.

Change has a much higher chance of occurring through transformative conversations. As a leader who nurtures those conversations, you can create and expand opportunities for change within your organization. It's important to empower team members to design effective change journeys that will work for all.

The goal is to create a team that responds to challenges with agility. The success of this effort is directly linked to employee buy in. Individuals involved in the design of a new idea are more likely to take ownership of it. Their vested interest will fuel their imagination for the future, and they will find ways to make that future happen.

A burning question: How can you facilitate change? The key lies in encouraging relationships and conversation. Individuals who participate in a system of making meaning together bind both society and organizations. Their dialogue enables understanding. Change results when people in conversation challenge meanings and construct new systems of working and relating.

The formal and informal communication networks that naturally develop in organizations largely determine the collective attitude that leads to change or stagnation. By nurturing change and facilitating dialogue, you will foster transformative conversations and cultural change. It's a powerful tool at the heart of your leadership journey.

Connection is critical

You are required to take concerted action for connection to occur. To prevent confusion, you need to understand three important terms: independence, dependence, and interdependence. These terms are widely misused in the context of leadership. It's useful to analyze their positive and negative implications. A richer understanding will lead to closer connections and better results.

Independence

When you think of independence, do images of freedom come to mind? Anything that is independent is not subject to bias, influence, or others' control. Independent people are self-directed, bold, and unconstrained. Most leaders like to think of themselves as independent. Used too often or sprinkled with arrogance, independence can lay a path to corruption, white-collar crime, and poor practices. Too much independence can lead to weak coordination and a lack of accountability.

Now flip the coin. Here's the positive. Leaders are rarely *totally* independent. The astute and effective leader, recognizing that self-evident truth from the Declaration of Independence that all men [and women] are created equal, treats others with respect. This kind of leader encourages independence of thought, self-direction, and self-control. This leader voluntarily tempers his or her independence with ethical values and concerns. The result is effective dialogue within the organization, as every participant has a platform to openly express independent thoughts while being equally sensitive to other's ideas.

Dependence

Dependence is obviously the opposite of independence, but it's worth examining. It is a state of relying on or being controlled by someone or something else. Oftentimes it's psychologically or physically habit-forming, like in the case of drugs or alcohol. The word dependence gets its bad rap because it's often linked to drug or emotional dependence.

The person who becomes dependent on the good graces of a difficult boss is often the laughing stock of coworkers. Society tends to scoff at those who are financially dependent.

For all of its negative connotations, there is an up side. Trusting in someone or something can yield fantastic results. As a leader, you certainly depend on others for your organization to be profitable and efficient. Being trustworthy and encouraging trustworthiness in others is vital for a successful leadership experience.

Interdependence

If you're having a hard time imaging an interdependent person, you're not alone. Think of it this way: an interdependent person is mutually dependent on another person. They depend on each other. It's being mutually responsible to and sharing a value set with others. It's different than dependence in that an interdependent relationship suggests all parties are emotionally, financially, or morally linked. Interdependence weaves families, societies, and organizations together.

The wise leader creates interconnectedness – collaboration – within the organization. The leader views the organization as a body, where each part is interdependent. That body requires all parts for survival and optimal health. This kind of thinking assigns importance to every part, and the optimal relationship between all the parts makes the body more efficient. It's the very essence of effective communication as a dialogue.

Some of history's greatest leaders advocated for interdependence. Their thought-provoking words add insight to the concept:

> "Interdependence is and ought to be as much the ideal of man as self-sufficiency. Man is a social being." – Mahatma Gandhi

> "The basic thought that guides these specific means of national recovery is not narrowly nationalistic. It is the insistence, as a first consideration, upon the interdependence of the various elements in all parts of the United States." – Franklin D. Roosevelt

"We are caught in an inescapable network of mutuality, tied in a single garment of destiny. Whatever affects one directly, affects all indirectly." – Martin Luther King Jr.

"Independent thinking alone is not suited to interdependent reality. Independent people who do not have the maturity to think and act interdependently may be good individual producers, but they won't be good leaders or team players." – Stephen Covey

"A hundred times every day I remind myself that my inner and outer life depend on the labors of other men, living and dead, and that I must exert myself in order to give in the same measure as I have received and am still receiving." – Albert Einstein

The collaborative spirit is the tie that binds these quotes together. Collaboration is made possible through dialogue, where everyone learns from each other and enriches their thinking and leadership in the process. It's important to rediscover and nurture connections with others, addressing some of the fragmentation that's characteristic to modern life. The practice will bring coherence to interpersonal relationships and foster an environment of appreciation. Once that environment exists, people can freely listen to each other and explore possibilities.

The magic happens when a group wanders into new territory and likes it. This new territory offers paths to fresh meaning and discoveries. Those paths, hidden from individuals, are accessible to the group. As individuals become vulnerable and share stories, hearts, and thoughts, new meanings flow from the whole group strengthening their creative capacity. This powerful experience of creating shared meaning is an important step toward collaboration.

It is possible for wise leaders to thrive in these new territories with their teams. By encouraging transformative conversations and leading through dialogue, healthy organizations can emerge. The process requires you to invite others into conversation. It may feel awkward to invite this living, reactive system – your team – into open conversation because of its unpredictability. Nevertheless, this journey of discovery can positively impact your personal growth and stimulate individuals to perform at new levels.

You will witness the power of dialogue as each participant's thoughts, questions, and opinions influence others. This continuous flow of meaning will provide important feedback and lead to mutual adaptation and clarity for the group. The give-and-take process will foster better understanding of each other and the situation. Understanding will lead to collaboration and transformation.

Your social brain

Most people think of their brain as an individual biological organ. They own it. They possess the thoughts, feelings, and opinions it produces. It's common to hear people say things like "I have to make up my own mind." Maybe you've said it yourself. Social neuroscience says that's not entirely true. It suggests the human brain is a social organ, always connecting to other brains.

This has huge implications for leading through dialogue considering advancements in understanding the neural infrastructure of social connection: attunement and empathy. This science provides a more powerful lens to explore the deep structures of human relationships. All of this suggests you don't always make up your own mind after all.

Human beings are a social bunch. Brains connect to other brains. Through the process of storytelling, dialogue, and other connecting activities humans have a way to download aspects of their surroundings to the brain. Data from the environment, culture, climate, and knowledge all play a role. Brains adapt, and in doing so the social brain of an organization can form the social synapse.

Think of the brain as a hub of energy connected to other brains. At the biological level the neurons that fire together, wire together. At the sociological level brains that think together, bond together. The brain, structured to adapt to its environment, provides a bridge for more efficient leadership.

Even though all of these highly effective bridges to creativity and efficiency exist, personal beliefs and thoughts can inhibit brain adaptation. As a leader, it's critical to open your mind to other influences. It's important to encourage others to share in this practice. With open mind channels, powerful paradigm shifts can occur. When those channels are closed, it's impossible to make others change their thinking, even though they may change their behavior. Behavior change does not necessarily indicate a true mind shift.

Lead with your social brain

Two characteristics of strong leaders are flexibility and openness. These attributes encourage the open exchange of opinions, analysis, and fruitful dialogue. They permit leaders to be vulnerable and without fully abandoning his or her stance, tell others "You're right; I didn't consider that angle." Flexible leaders have the ability to maturely fine-tune their opinions, based on the valuable input of others.

When you show empathy, understanding, and the willingness to listen to diverse opinions, the mirror neurons of other brains will follow suit. Mirror neurons are a special class of brain cells that fire not only when an individual performs an action, but also when the individual observes someone else make the same movement. When you smile and conduct business in a kind, ethical manner, chances are the mirror neurons of team members' will elicit a similar response.

The most powerful, profound changes will result when all of the brains in the group are in sync. Diverse minds offer diverse ways of thinking and creating. Brains firing together also help prevent oversights and mistakes. This kind of neurodiversity is critical for change to occur. This leadership model requires you to promote idea sharing, rather than rely on what you "know."

You'll be most successful when you believe and acknowledge that you don't have all the answers. Wider perspectives will allow ideas to emerge naturally, resulting in a rich array of solutions and strategies. True wisdom arises not only from personal intellect, but also from a larger source within each person. It manifests in the collective social brain.

Think about your own leadership style. Size up your social brain. You will likely excel if you accept that you don't know everything and rely on the collective social brain to thrive. The opposite is also true. If you lead alone, relying solely on what you personally know, the path to success will be rocky at best. When different brains come together in collaboration, the end result will be wiser, and survival will be most likely to happen.

The social brain likes company as much as it likes to share thoughts. Your employees will bond if you give them the opportunity to collaborate and think together in dialogue.

Brains that think together bond together. Your role is to facilitate the interaction of the brains around you. Don't just make people *feel* they are part of the business, *make* them part of the growing and evolving future business, from planning to implementation. Their brains will bond and the reward will be a positive and productive environment.

You have a social brain. Use it wisely to connect and construct a stronger business and better world.

Collaboration wins the day

Collaboration means joining together to accomplish that which cannot be realized alone. As the old adage says, "Many hands make light work." The power of collaboration is well illustrated through a childhood experience of mine in Cuba. I'll never forget it. I was in a Jeep with my parents and their two friends. We were off to a meeting in a neighboring community. The rain came just as we approached an isolated and rough dirt road. While crossing a small stream, one of our tires plunged into a deep hole. Despite our attempts to lift and push the vehicle, it wouldn't budge.

Light rain soon turned to a torrential downpour. In consternation we watched the stream convert to a swift-running river. For the next few hours, I envisioned our Jeep being swept away in the current. Thankfully, several men from nearby farms came to our rescue with their horses. We joined forces in collaboration, pulled the vehicle free, and escaped danger.

In this same spirit, you can help your organization get unstuck and move forward by combining individual gifts, strengths, and ideas. You can create the momentum to move everyone forward in the desired direction. Envision a series of gears, where the cogs align and leverage the energies of each gear. Now picture each member of your team as one of those gears. If one gear is misaligned, forward progress will be difficult. Your goal is to identify strengths and keep the gears running smoothly by facilitating clear communication through dialogue. The stronger the connection, the easier it will be to move together toward transformation.

Have you heard the concept of the learning organization? It goes like this when applied to dialogue. When your focus is on organizational transformation, your goal is to bring fundamental change to functions within that organization. It requires you and your team to abandon former ways of handling business so new behaviors can form. When transformative learning happens for individuals who are joining together to meet goals, that energy bubbles up to the organizational level. The result is organizational transformation.

The heart of connection starts with you

Connections keep the tapestry of life strong and healthy. This unique energy sparks between people when they feel seen, heard, valued, and validated. It's strongest when people exchange openly and without judgment. As a result, they gain strength from the human exchange. Wholehearted conversations take individuals across the spectrum to genuine connection.

What happens when the fibers of these conversations are inauthentic? Oftentimes, business failures and unethical practices have their roots in a lack of authentic dialogue. Leaders must know and understand themselves before they can address others. It requires them to have clear thoughts and goals. Only then can conversations spring from the authentic self. Others will recognize it, and it will resonate.

To develop this kind of connection, you must first expose your legitimate self and accept others in their purest forms. Remove the mask. Speak from the heart. Share your thoughts and feelings with integrity. When you are authentic and true to your values and convictions, your value as a leader will be evident. Unmistakably so.

The real story on authenticity

It's easy to tell people to "be authentic," but what does authenticity mean? At its core, authenticity is about being true. To yourself. Your family. Your friends. Your colleagues. Your customers. Everyone. It's about presenting yourself in a genuine way. No pretense. No make-believe life. It requires you to read your own mind. That might sound strange, but it actually makes perfect sense.

As people search for meaning and happiness in their personal and professional lives, they must be real with themselves first. Have the hard talks in their own heads. Be completely raw with their thoughts. Participate in the present. It plays out differently for people based on their own perspectives on authenticity. Existentialists go so far as to believe that inauthentic people can fall into chronic anxiety, boredom, and despair.

Leaders tend to display their authenticity in one of two ways. There are leaders who are authentic to themselves, their values, hopes, dreams, and self-development. Other leaders are authentic to the situation, or the context in which they find themselves. Leaders who seek others' approval and dance to the tune of public recognition should heed caution. In the words of William Shakespeare's Polonius in Hamlet "This above all: to thine own self be true, and it must follow, as the night the day, thou canst not then be false to any man."

How authentic are you? What does authenticity mean for your leadership style? Are you the real deal? A bona fide, sincere you? Are you thriving in a state of healthy alignment between your values and behaviors? Ask yourself these questions as you journey toward authenticity. It's a highly coveted leadership quality, and a bridge to knowledge, growth, and learning. Here are four ways to strengthen your authenticity:

1. Know yourself

What issues do you grapple with in daily life? Are they issues about others, or are they about you and your reaction to others? You react to people based on your past experiences and values. You must be yourself to be an effective leader. This requires you to know yourself. This is key because people want to be led by a person, not a title on a business card.

In June 2005 *Leadership Quarterly* dedicated a special issue to authentic leadership. In the lead article, Gardner, Avolio, Luthans, May, and Walumba said increasing self-awareness was key to developing authentic leadership, and that authentic leaders are "more aware of, and committed to, their core end values." In the same journal, Avolio and Gardner said, "Self-awareness is an appropriate starting point for interpreting what constitutes authentic leadership development."

Do not expect self-awareness to emerge overnight. Do plan for an ongoing process where you continually come to terms with your skills, core values, and sense of purpose. It's a journey of understanding what you care about most in your personal and professional life. You can achieve the process through dedication. Today's complex world imposes an array of choices and distractions. It takes stamina to sift through to what's important.

2. Know what you know, and what you don't

Of course you know what you know, and you know what you don't know. Right? Wrong. Admit it. There are times when you willingly choose to ignore facts. Take for instance that business partner who is sabotaging your efforts. You've been friends for ages, so you shrug off what's obvious to others. If it's not your business partner, maybe it's a vendor. An employee. Someone on your board. The point is, you may experience this knowing as a feeling. You can't actually put your finger on how you know you're being sabotaged, so you push the thought away when it creeps into your mind. Dismiss. Delete. Poof. Gone into your subconscious. Now you forget you know. A better strategy is to address the feeling and have a mature conversation with yourself first, and then speak with the person in question.

Do you want to get to the bottom of something that's nagging you? To find facts? It's your responsibility to seek that information in any way possible. Once you track down the information, deep transformative learning can occur. Take time to reflect, learn from the experience, and integrate your newfound knowledge into your personal value set.

3. Know what you want

Do you know what you want in life? Surprisingly, many people are clueless. They take what comes their way. They hope it all works out. Bad idea. You must have clarity on your goals and needs for the outcomes to align accordingly. For the dream to come true. If you know exactly what you want, you will be energized and empowered to go get it. Success will come easier; the journey will be more enjoyable.

Some people endure painstaking struggle to get what they think they want. Then they're disappointed. The prize isn't so sweet. This occurs because they didn't have a clear picture of what they truly desired. More importantly, they didn't think through the ramifications. Take time to reflect on what you want. Think about it in great detail. Assess the side effects of getting it. This will make for a more focused, effective, and rewarding life.

4. Know how to align who you are, what you live, and how you lead

When everything clicks together – who you are, your lifestyle, your leadership style – your authenticity will shine. To align your values and behaviors, first evaluate your stated values as they relate to your active values. Do not pretend. Do you practice what you preach? Do you preach what you practice?

At times you may feel drained of your energy and enthusiasm. Maybe you're suffering from a struggle between your beliefs and behaviors. This can hurt your performance and make profitability plummet. It can ignite morale issues within your team. To achieve your peak performance, it's critical to bring your real, fully engaged self to work. You will be successful to the degree that who you are and what you live are aligned.

Put it all together

A colleague and I had an impactful conversation regarding a leader she was coaching. As you read this summary, think about his journey toward authenticity, and how it relates to your own leadership experience. Here's how she presented it to me.

> A leader I'm coaching has a big heart, but a cold exterior. He has a reputation for being – his words – " a mean asshole." He's responsible for two new divisions. Before, just one. He assumes the new people he'll be working with are probably crying due to his arrival. He's at a loss for how to handle the situation.

I advised her to get straight to the point with her client. This leader should be real and come clean with his new team. He should tell his employees that he is aware of his reputation. He must take the opportunity to share what he stands for and discuss his commitment to the team. It's his chance to explain his perspective, values, and vision in his own words. He shouldn't hold back.

My colleague later shared with me that her client followed up in exactly that manner. He had considered multiple ways to handle the situation, but none of his scenarios included him sharing his authentic self. As he shifted his perceptive, he realized the value in being real. He experienced the process and value of walking the line close to vulnerability, but not stepping on it. It made him transparent. Real.

Some of the most authentic leaders highlight the importance of congruence in their personal leadership styles. They mention the fear of becoming stagnant and their need to grow. After all, they can't expect others to grow if they're not modeling the behavior. Other leaders make sure their style is in lockstep with their philosophical views.

The common factors of authenticity, sincerity, and high integrity foster transformative learning. As authenticity encourages honesty, dialogue results. Then meaning making occurs. This process, which starts with the leader, encourages genuineness and openness in others. The workplace becomes more humane, fulfilling, creative, and ultimately productive.

As you strive to lead authentically, think of it as a process that occurs from the inside out. You must first have the internal willingness and courage to take risks and make mistakes. As you become aware of your shortcomings, you will quickly spot them in action. Then you'll learn from them. As you allow yourself to be vulnerable, you will acknowledge your interdependence on others. Then you will begin to search for what is best and unique. You will learn to value learning, yet never fully knowing; being curious, yet nimble when surprises come your way. You will see yourself as a constant work in progress.

Harness heart power

Heart power. It's a profound concept, as leading from the heart can move mediocre results to big success. Research conducted by The Center for Creative Leadership concluded that the ability to care for and understand what others are feeling is a statistically significant factor in the success of the best leaders.

The heart reaches out for connection. There's a scientific basis that explains why the heart plays a leading role in our relationships. It offers insight into how the heart impacts mental clarity, creativity, emotional balance, and personal effectiveness. In the 1990s, scientists in the emerging field of neurocardiology discovered that people have a true brain in the heart. It acts independently of the head. It has more than 40,000 nerve cells, a complex network of neurotransmitters, and ways to influence the brain's chemistry.

The electrical energy in the heart creates a powerful magnetic field around the heart. Recent studies have found that the coherence of the heart brain's rhythms can dramatically change the effectiveness of the thinking brain in the head. The heart brain is a real, powerful force.

You can harness this heart power to arrive at better results. According to Bill George, a Harvard Professor, author, and researcher "The best leaders are not the 'follow me over the hill' type, rather, they're the people who lead from the heart as well as the head, and whose leadership style springs from their fundamental character and values. It is the leaders that empower others and create leaders that are the most successful and profitable."

What does this mean for you? Unless you can feel values and goals deeply in your heart, you can't live them. It's your heart, not your head, which plays the dominant role in moving you to excel and connect within your organization. The brain in your heart is searching for opportunities to grow and learn. It's radar for uncovering significant connection points.

Learn to lead from your heart

People are motivated when their hearts are touched, when they're inspired, and when they experience a sense of purpose. Leaders can use all of this to their advantage in creating connections. Rather than pushing the team to complete tasks, the wise leader will invite people to participate in an attitude of partnership. For this reason, leading through transformative conversations is the heart of the leadership journey.

Think about the most memorable leaders. The best of the best. What was remarkable about them? What did they accomplish? Chances are they found a way to bind their hearts to others' hearts. They took relationships to heart. They used stories and personal sharing. They listened and encouraged dialogue. They knew that strong heart connections drove performance. They realized the power of inspired motivation as they watched individuals connect their daily practices with their guiding beliefs. These leaders watched their teams perform well in the face of obstacles.

You can lead from the heart if you learn to listen to it. Rather than base your actions on what others say, instead act based on what your heart tells you. When there is conflict between your actions and what you believe in your heart, you will wage an internal war. You will have a congruent life when you listen to your heart and follow it. It will be less stressful, and more peaceful.

When was the last time you listened to your heart? Did you give it your full attention? Ignoring it brings danger. It's easy to silence it though, considering the people and things clamoring for your attention. Listening closely can be inconvenient. Scary at times. But definitely worth it. Follow these steps to listen to your heart:

1. Make time to be alone and quiet.
2. Ignore voices that tell you what you should or shouldn't do.
3. De-clutter your over-thinking file.
4. Remove your justifications.
5. Release your judgments.
6. Practice.

It takes extreme courage to follow your heart's voice even when it doesn't make logical sense. When you listen to your heart, you stop analyzing facts and figures and instead hear the story of your evolving self. Only then will you begin to truly understand and live your values. You will be compassionate with yourself and others. You will find yourself making the right ethical choices and valuing your relationships. The end result is a more compassionate leader. You.

This epiphany will expose your truest values and morals. They live deep in your heart. Reflect. Look inside and ask yourself:

- How do I feel?
- What do I see?
- What are my key values?
- What is my vision for life and work?

- What kind of life, work environment, and relationships do I want to create or enrich?
- Where can I make a difference?
- What makes me feel good, connected, and involved?

As you examine your answers, consider how following your heart can aid in your daily decision-making and personal interactions. Leading from the heart through transformative conversations will become second nature. As you begin to relate to others in this new way, a caring quality will emerge from your leadership style. The service and contributions you bestow on others will ultimately serve the common good.

The most effective leaders in today's organizations engage in actions that are directly connected to their own values and ideals. To their hearts. They have a strong sense of purpose. They help others define meaning. They build connections by nurturing transformative conversations. This helps people create meaning together. It ignites connection and community.

2 Barriers to Transformative Conversations

W<small>E ALL KNOW</small> the frustration of hitting a barrier. A roadblock. An obstruction. A stoppage. It prevents progress and limits access. When there's a barrier to dialogue, something prevents a meeting of meaning. Most dialogue barriers arise when opinions and worldviews clash. As human beings, we have an innate need to protect and affirm our beliefs. This behavior can threaten others and drive us to lead lives of self-justification. It can result in defensive behavior and uneasy situations. When these situations escalate, it can be difficult to speak openly or hear honestly. The manifestation of this fundamental concern for one's being is a meaning barrier.

Whether you think of them as conversational breakdowns, structural traps, or potholes, meaning barriers can be difficult to avoid. However, you can learn how to spot them and take alternate routes. Here are a dozen common barriers with suggestions for breaking through them:

1. Language

Language is complex. People can hear words differently and assign multiple meanings based on the personal emotions they have experienced in association with those words. Dialogue can be compromised if specific meanings are not explored and clarified. In 1975, Kantor and Lehr, scholars and co-authors of *Inside the Family*, introduced the concept of three different languages – the languages of feeling, meaning, and power – that people use to express themselves. Because each person tends to default to his or her preferred language, most dialogues use one of these three languages

Those who speak the language of feeling are primarily concerned with how people feel. They see the world as a network of relationships. They cue in to both the tone and content of expressions. People who speak the language of meaning express interest in values, theory, and philosophy. Ideas are their passion. Inquiry ignites their spirits. Finally, individuals who speak the language of power simply want direction. In this context, power means the energy to get things done.

Everyone has a preferred language mode to communicate and receive everyday information. Since we receive information through the senses, the three preferences are visual, kinesthetic, and auditory. We are generally stronger in two of them, and weaker in a third. The closer your language is to the other person's preferred method of receipt, the easier you will be understood.

For example, if you are stronger in the visual mode, you'll tend to use phrases like "let's see how it goes" or "watch for mistakes." If you are stronger in the kinesthetic mode, your language will include words like build, grasp, move, score, and touch. If you prefer the auditory mode, your words will include click, hear, ring, tell, and discuss.

If people are not aware of their language tendencies and differences, there could be a serious dialogue breakdown. Think about your own conversations. Do you ever feel that others are missing your point? Do they look at you as if you've missed theirs? It's all too common. The next time you're in a dialogue that's dominated by one of the three languages, open new doors of understanding by exploring the other languages.

Break the Barrier: Don't assume you know. Explore the meaning of words to feel confident everyone understands what is being discussed. It will be worth the effort.

2. Images

We all know a picture is worth a thousand words. This is why images play such a key role in communication. The images people have of each other or the subject matter being discussed can influence dialogue. Favorable images can help promote the success of the dialogue. Negative images can lead to disaster.

We are great at filling in blanks. Sometimes it works to our disadvantage. Barriers can emerge as we filter what people say through our perception of them, or what we think they believe or are attempting to say. Have you ever brought your preconceptions to dialogue? If you filtered the discussion through images, chances are good distortion was the result.

Break the Barrier: Create opportunities for people to know each other. Remind others to suspend assumptions and judgments. Release images from past experiences and help clarify distortions.

3. Anxieties

Anxiety comes in many forms. People have personal anxieties. Subject matter anxieties. Interpersonal anxieties. These anxieties can create barriers and diminish learning and dialogue opportunities. It is difficult for an anxious person to fully engage another person. Anxiety can lead to fear, and that can prompt defensive behavior. None of which leads to productive dialogue.

Does your busy schedule ever cause anxiety? Is crunch time a source of underlying nervousness? You're not alone. For dialogue to work, you must be willing to relinquish your anxieties and invest enough in others for the process of dialogue to unfold.

Break the Barrier: Anxiety is contagious. So is calmness. You can thank your brain's mirror neurons for both. If you can exhibit calmness, those in your company will likely calm down too. Keep the rhythm of dialogue slow enough to open a calm space for sharing. If you amp up, first breathe, then step back and ask clarifying questions to quell your fears and anxiety.

4. Defensiveness

Defensiveness blocks dialogue. It reveals itself in less-than-pretty ways. Defensive behavior often shows itself through self-justification, prejudices, compulsive talking, denial, distortion, and projection, to name a few. People in defensive mode are closed off to entertaining concepts. This stance makes it nearly impossible to explore others' thoughts, ideas, and feelings. People typically become defensive when they think others disagree with their viewpoints.

Break the Barrier: Set aside your own certainties and insecurities and open yourself to receive others' thoughts and opinions. Rather than listening with your guard up, let the meaning of others' words flow fluidly through your tightly guarded opinions and judgments.

5. Holding back

Presenter stands at the podium in the front. Participants fill in the seats in the back. It's so common it's laughable. Many people hold back when it comes to participating. Obviously, leaders want exactly the opposite. They want robust, stimulating dialogue that furthers thoughts and meaning. It's impossible to achieve this when participants hold back. In fact, the most common complaint among leaders who want to use dialogue is that their team members hold back and avoid participation.

You've likely heard all the excuses, from the common to the creative. There's the person who "doesn't feel comfortable enough to speak in this group." Then there's the one who "doesn't want his words to come back to bite him." Let's not forget the employee who wants to "see how it goes" before she inserts her opinions. People often find it difficult to become involved when they're afraid of how others might react. Their ideas might be met with hostility, or dismissed as irrelevant. You can overcome these barriers and alleviate embarrassment by building trust with participants.

Break the Barrier: Learn to discern what is true for you, and then trust yourself to introduce your thoughts to the group. Lean into your discomfort. Speak up. Repeat.

6. Contrary views and purposes

We've all met *that* person. The one whose sole mission in life is to adopt a contrary viewpoint to anything and everything. The consummate devil's advocate. These folks argue for the sake of argument. They convert dialogue into a game of wits. How exactly does this play out? When one person wants to establish and secure agreement, the other person pushes to explore options. The result is contrary purpose. This push-and-pull interaction interferes with the pursuit of mutual understanding. It can be exhausting.

Sometimes what seems like a contrary view is only a difference in information processing. Some people are more sequential in their thinking, focusing on content, details, organization, logic, accuracy, and tasks. Others think more globally, focusing on context, the big picture, strategic planning and implementation, innovation, systemic thinking, and innovation. Still others are integrated with a near-equal balance between sequential and global strengths. The business world demands diversity of thinking for optimal outcomes.

Break the Barrier: A certain amount of contrary thinking can expand thoughts, explanations, ideas, and choices. If it becomes obstructive, let it go and bring curiosity back with open questions. Remember that diversity of thought results in better decision making.

7. Monologue

Some speakers are so preoccupied and fascinated with themselves that they actually lose self-awareness. The audience fades into a fog. The monologue continues. Within the dance of dialogue, one partner – the audience – begins to stand still while the other partner – the speaker – continues to boogie on down. It's as awkward as it sounds. Within these situations, there is no openness. No space for shared inquiry. No creativity. It is a monopoly of a single perspective. The speaker is focused on protecting personal views and convincing others of the absolute correctness of those views.

When taken to the extreme, the speaker slips into denial. He forgets the audience has equal rights. He believes others' views are unfounded. Crazy. Baseless. Consequently, no listening to responses can possibly occur. People begin to talk to themselves. The conversation becomes repetitious. It goes nowhere.

Break the Barrier: It is unfair and immature for one person to occupy the stage for too long. Remind yourself and others that dialogue becomes richer when there's an open space for everyone to share ideas and perspectives. Force yourself to listen more, talk less.

8. Assumptions

Throughout the course of life, everyone builds up some assumptions about self, others, and the world in general. They are the product of years of past experiences and observations. These assumptions are layered with biases. If people are unable to bring their assumptions to the forefront of dialogue, and to examine and discuss them, they slip into the unconscious. Hidden. Suppressed. Slipping out in unproductive ways. Shooting down dialogue.

Have you ever thought you know what another person is thinking and feeling, and then reacted with your assumption? We are all guilty of this. It happens when we don't give others the chance to clarify meaning. It is one of the most common roadblocks you'll encounter. Perhaps it's your greatest area for personal growth. This behavior, which can almost feel reflexive, can sabotage dialogue.

Within a dialogue, if you assume others will not understand your point of view you may not even bother to explain your thinking. If you don't feel the remotest possibility of having collaboration within your department, you won't even try. Why waste the energy, right? Wrong. When assumptions take the status of fact and truth, dialogue suffers greatly. It will lead to ineffectiveness, conflict, and lack of learning. The inability to think creatively vanishes.

Break the Barrier: Rather than reacting based on your assumptions, use suspension and inquiry to bring assumptions to the surface. Repeatedly encourage others to suspend their assumptions. Then make conscious choices about which ones are real and helpful, and which ones should be dismissed.

9. Timing

Waiting for the perfect moment to speak can be paralyzing. On one hand, the impulse to make a point before absorbing or pondering what has been said can bring pressure to talk too soon. On the other hand, mulling things over for so long that the conversation shifts focus can make your comment irrelevant. There's a subtle balance between jumping in too fast and holding back too much. There's a craft to knowing when to speak.

Timing also has to do with moving to action prematurely. Jumping the gun. This is especially prevalent in the United States. Employee groups frequently complain of using too much time to talk. They like quick results. Instant gratification. An action plan to get it done. Ample time spent in dialogue allows individuals to probe thoughts and feelings. Taking time to let this process unfold leads to wiser decisions and more strategic action plans.

Break the Barrier: Don't let others' impatience for action, or your own, sabotage understanding and relationship building. It's important to recognize that dialogue is part of the action. Listen within and outside of yourself. What is flowing within the group? When a question or feeling pushes into your awareness, that's your cue to speak.

10. Taking action

I once facilitated a three-day meeting in Iceland for a diverse group of engineers who were part of a multinational manufacturing organization. Many of them had recently been assigned to a new division within the company. They liked to take action, not talk. Not surprisingly, managers spent two years struggling to unite objectives, push innovation forward, and collaborate without much success.

On the first day, our group of 60 got to know one another through activities and conversations in mixed groups. It was the first time many of them felt like they were on the same team. During the subsequent days, participants found ways to collaborate and take specific team action toward the future. People shared vital information. They displayed real energy. The leader later told me more progress was made in those three days than in the entire two years prior. Some participants would have loved to take action from the outset, but most attendees understood that building relationships led to progress.

Break the Barrier: For people to take effective action, they need to know and trust each other, plus understand what needs to happen. They must also take ownership in planning and implementation. Assign time for this process to evolve. What may feel like a slow start will accelerate the success of your actions.

11. Structural traps

According to W. Isaacs, who pioneered the use of dialogue in organizations, "Structures are composed of the quality, content, and timeliness of the information being conveyed. This includes the goals, incentives, costs, and feedback that motivate or constrain behavior." With that in mind, structural traps occur when one part of a system encourages people to act one way, while another part demands contradictory behavior.

For example, an organization may promote flexible work hours, but meanwhile individual supervisors may watch clocks and evaluate staff accordingly. Dilemmas surface when the parts of a system are not synchronized or communicating properly. These underlying issues, often unspoken, can be perpetuated and lead to organizational dysfunction.

Break the Barrier: To truly identify and address unspoken issues and structural traps, convene stakeholders from all parts of the system. Facilitate an open dialogue about uncomfortable issues. Structural issues can only be repaired and strengthened when all voices are present.

12. Egos

Ego can impede progress. They can creep in without warning. Imagine a work group trying to solve a business problem. An easy one. Yet they're stuck. The sticking point may not have anything to do with a lack of funds, talent, or capacity. It may have everything to do with ego. Too much ego from too many people. It's often the case that the real problem is really never the problem. Almost invariably the real problem is an overdose of ego. Whether it's two toddlers fighting for the same toy, two countries warring over borders, or two executives entrenched in their individual positions, it all boils down to one thing. Too much ego.

Leaders who can't resist the temptation to show off are simply feeding their egos. Academics are often guilty of the same behavior. The bigger the egos, the quicker the breakdown in dialogue. Dialogue requires humility and a willingness to empathize with someone else's point of view. Leaders who pride themselves on having the last word dismiss other viewpoints as a result. They focus on their own agendas and needs instead of finding what is best for the group. Productive dialogue cannot thrive in the presence of inflated egos.

Break the Barrier: Become intimately familiar with your ego. Be poised to send it packing so you can concentrate on finding solid solutions. When you're facilitating a dialogue between big egos, nurture weaker voices and provide opportunities for discussion. Be prepared to tactfully ignore the incessant talker and gently invite comments from others. Because ego management can be daunting, remind yourself to focus on these five items:

- Focus on the problem. Gain clarity and remember that it's not about you.
- Focus on results. Identify desired outcomes and benefits of solving the problem.
- Focus on understanding. Open a genuine dialogue so sharing can occur.
- Focus on solutions. Get to solutions sooner rather than later, and hone in on the best ideas.
- Focus on implementation. Create an action plan so issues don't fester.

13. Fixed ideas

It can be hard to shake off "the best idea in the world." When people become obsessed with a fixed idea or interest, they're often blind to other concepts. They move full-steam ahead on a one-way track. In the process, they become incapable of absorbing other knowledge or concepts.

In today's society, many people get stuck on predictable and well-publicized themes. For example, gender equality, childhood obesity and energy conservation are top-of-mind in the social psyche. These trending topics receive a lot of superficial attention, but individuals may not be motivated to pursue deeper understanding or solutions. While preoccupation with these topics can certainly be justified, trouble ensues when people approach them with entrenched viewpoints, rather than in the spirit of dialogue.

Break the Barrier: Let others articulate their viewpoints and take their concerns seriously, even if you're opposed. This creates an environment where others feel you hear and understand them. If you are holding a fixed idea, put it by the wayside. While you can make it your personal mission, don't let it clog the airwaves and obstruct the free flow of ideas.

Encourage interaction

If you noticed, most of the suggestions on how to break barriers involved some kind of interaction. After you grow accustomed to identifying and breaking through these barriers, dialogue will have the opportunity to flow freely. However, successful dialogue also calls for a high level of interaction. Here are some effective methods for encouraging interaction:

Glance around

Within a dialogue, people speak to the group as a whole. This calls for scanning, rather than direct one-on-one eye contact. When you speak, glance around the group. People will follow suit. Soon enough, the whole group will give more attention to the subject matter and the group than to individuals. Glancing around also helps discourage the tendency for the conversation to drift into monologues.

Look for signs

As you glance around, be on the lookout for people who appear puzzled, anxious, distraught, or ready to blurt comments. As one person concludes a thought, you will be positioned to draw in a less vocal participant. You can say, "Pam, I saw you frowning when Paul was talking. Do you want to share your thoughts?"

Cues can be subtle. Indrawn breathing. Snorts. Eye rolls. Head nods. Note them and let people see you doing so. It will keep interaction alive. It will also keep you tuned into the climate of the group. As you look for signals, you may even give the group a better sense of its identity.

Give green lights, red lights

Some people participate. Others observe. Invite observes into the discussion. You can do it verbally or non-verbally. On the other hand, you may need to restrain an overactive participant. The person who constantly talks or interrupts can disrupt the group's equilibrium. Mitigate frustration by handling it in a supportive and straightforward way. You can say, "Could you wait Brian? It would be interesting to hear how others respond to that." Or try, "Hold your comment there for the moment, Liz. Let's hear what someone else has to offer." Handling it this way will provide relief to the group, while not unduly putting out the dominant participant.

Reflect and deflect questions

Resist the urge to set yourself up as an expert. You may receive questions like, "Can you tell us what you know about…?" or, "What's the answer?" Slip out of this trap by reflecting the question back on the person. You can say, "Well, what do you think?" In most cases, the person has an idea of the answer. It's best to let participants formulate their own ideas. That said, there may be times when you are the only one who knows the answer to a particular question. If this happens, or if refusing to answer the question will slow down proceedings, definitely offer feedback.

It can also be useful to deflect questions. Someone may say, "I don't understand what the CEO is trying to say with that email. What does it all mean?" You can deflect with, "Does anyone else have the same feeling? Can anyone decipher the meaning?"

Provide value and support

Remember, it's crucial for people to feel safe and to build relationships. Dialogue demands an atmosphere of trust. It calls for openness. People need to feel valued for who they are so they don't fear ridicule and embarrassment. Do not correct contributions or encourage the belief that there are right and wrong answers to every question. The dialogue will deteriorate if you become the judge of right and wrong.

If a participant is way off base, expand the conversation. Invite further thought. Encourage more participation. You can say, "Let's take a moment to think about that again." Another option is to ask, "How does that relate to what we've already discussed?" These comments will trigger people to realize that they've said something irrelevant or inconsistent. It's a great way to let them redeem themselves.

Check and build

Group work can cause people to loose confidence. They might not be as lucid as they desire. Some of the most imaginative contributors may find it difficult to express their half-formed ideas with clarity. To prevent confusion within the group, do a quick check for understanding and meaning. Say something like, "Let me make sure I understand you. Are you saying…?" The person will be grateful. The group will be relieved.

Help people identify connections and build understanding with a comment like, "That ties in well with the point Daniel made earlier." You can also ask, "Does that contradict what you said a few minutes ago?" It's always preferable for participants to make their own interpretations. To stimulate those connections say, "How does that connect with what you said before?" You may want to put emerging themes together, but it's more effective to encourage reflection when everyone can experience it together.

Redirect

People veer off topic. Discussions get bogged down. Sometimes it's necessary to change course. You can redirect a conversation by saying, "Our conversation doesn't feel productive. I think we've reached a point where we can turn our attention to…" Yet, in the spirit of dialogue, there's even a more open way to approach the problem. You can turn to the group and say, "Do you think we've worked on that one long enough now?" It may be valuable to check the process as well as content by saying, "Can we do a quick check to make sure we're going about this correctly?"

Regardless of your technique for encouraging interaction, the objective is to have as much input as possible. You will become skilled at assessing energy levels. The conversation's rhythm will prompt you to pause or move to a new topic or question. As your facilitation skills develop, you will gain incremental satisfaction with the quality of your transformative conversations.

3 *Facilitating Transformative Conversation*

DIALOGUE THAT ELICITS change is powerful. Who you are, what you do, and the way you present yourself in dialogue leads to success or failure. But, there's more at play. The elements needed for successful dialogue include: mutuality, listening, respect, suspension of judgment, trust, confidentiality, and a positive relationship. Think of dialogue as a protective container where intense emotions can safely emerge. Creative transformation takes place in this container.

I did not have access to these elements while growing up in communist Cuba. I had no freedom of expression. Publishing anything required approval. In school, teachers wanted to hear official answers. I could not say anything critical to authority figures. It was stifling. My mouth was in prison. I suspect government officials feared freedom of expression. Maybe they realized the power of dialogue. Perhaps they knew it would bring people together and expand possibilities for creating meaning and change.

Everything was different when I arrived in the United States. It was a delight to communicate freely. I studied everything I could on the topics of effective and open communication, change, and leadership. I was in love with communication. This affection spurred me to earn a doctoral degree in organizational behavior. Everyone must share my passion for speaking freely and exchanging ideas! Or so I thought.

Imagine my shock as I began to work with executives whose sentiments toward communication mirrored those of the communist government I left behind in Cuba. Was I hearing correctly? How could this happen in a country that prized – and had – freedom of speech? I realized that authoritarian leaders, whether in government or companies, create a logjam in the free flow of communication. Not surprisingly, these companies were the same ones to struggle with quality control and profitability. A suppressive environment is not conducive to dialogue. It leaves a slim chance for positive results.

When we engage in dialogue, meaning emanates from the group. Our whole being participates in an active relationship with others. Out of this emerges a possibility for newness, meaning making, and understanding. People can learn to reflect and talk together, even in the heat of challenging moments. Through this living experience of inquiry, they can explore hidden meanings, assumptions, values, and traps. It's an open-ended, dynamic process that promotes a stronger understanding of relationships.

Why don't all organizations harness the potential of dialogue? Many don't offer an environment where people feel safe to speak. Leaders don't encourage open communication or value collaboration. Employees don't have the skills or confidence to communicate effectively. They may talk to each other, but that's not true dialogue. For ideas to flow freely, dialogue must occur. Though there is no one method for dialogue, it has certain distinguishing elements worth exploring.

Space

Space suggests time and place. In the context of dialogue, timing is critical and space should be comfortable. However, it goes beyond that to a psychological space. Renowned physicist and theorist David Bohn encourages the importance of a free empty space "where we are not obliged to do anything, nor to come to any conclusions, nor to say anything or not say anything." We must be empty before we can hold something. Then we can reveal our innermost thoughts in authentic voices.

Today's fast-paced society tricks us into believing we do not have the time or prerogative to pause, be silent, think, and reflect. Run faster. Breathe harder. Repeat. It's a vicious cycle. It's not reality. We must pause. Silent reflection props open the mind's door long enough for new perceptions, ideas, and solutions to emerge. Conversations need breathing space. It's critical to slow down conversations so insights can occur in the space between words.

William Penn said, "True silence is the rest of the mind; it is to the spirit what sleep is to the body, nourishment and refreshment." The more emotionally loaded the subject matter, the greater the need for silent space. There are techniques you can use to gauge the need for silent space and for redirecting dialogue. Be aware of these signs, which indicate that a dialogue is deteriorating into a discussion. Observe and ask yourself if anyone is:

- Interrupting?
- Giving responses with little thought?
- Jumping to conclusions before gaining clarity?
- Formulating responses while others are speaking?
- Furthering a personal agenda?
- Talking in circles?
- Reiterating thoughts, without adding value?
- Monopolizing the conversation?
- Speaking without seeking input?
- Exhibiting defensive behavior?

You've probably observed all of these behaviors in your meetings. Reflect on the process and procedures that you use in dialogue and problem solving. This exercise will help you correct distortions and identify the strengths and weaknesses of your actions. Even if you feel too pressed for time to open space and pause, it is critical to hush the noise and connect with yourself and your team.

Dialogue requires you to pry open the "in between," a space where you can focus. A space to hear all the voices. A space to experience deep connection. A space to experience differences as gifts that can create a stronger result. A space to interrogate reality. A space to learn. A space to tackle challenges. A space to enrich relationships. A space where greater wisdom can emerge from the expression of all the voices in the group.

Safety

Dialogue can feel risky. Create a safe environment where dialogue can blossom. A safe place is where:

- *People can be vulnerable.* In doing so, they know others will embrace them, rather than exploit them.
- *There is a protective structure.* The group should work together to build ground rules that protect the process of dialogue. Individuals should feel confident that you will promote and enforce the guidelines.
- *People show respect.* When participants take each other seriously, they examine their peers' experiences. Screaming, attacks, and cursing are inexcusable. Check emotions.

Respect is the great equalizer. It requires participants to entertain all perspectives and listen to the many voices within themselves and others. At the same time, it calls for the discipline to silence the mind and ask thoughtful questions, entertain multiple ideas, and recognize the concept of equal rights and responsibilities.

When you respect other people, you must take them seriously and look for the source of their experience. Even when you do not agree with other people, or you find their perspectives unacceptable, you must accept their viewpoints as valid. Do not discount or belittle them. Instead, honor them and look for the sense in their words and thoughts.

When you practice respect, you acknowledge that you can learn from someone. It takes practice to develop the capacity to respect yourself and others, especially if they oppose you. Respect the polarizations that arise and resist the urge to "fix" others.

Respect opens a safe space for different perspectives and new meanings to emerge. The safety of true respect enables genuine inquiry and dialogue.

Mutuality

Dialogue requires a mutual quest for understanding where participants value each other as partners on a journey to new territory. One person's perspective may shift or change others' views. Each person has something to contribute, and something to receive. Learning together is key. If someone takes on the persona of teacher, mutuality is lost and dialogue disappears. Consequently, opportunities for creativity and change are lost.

In his discussion on symmetry, J. Habermas, a German philosopher and sociologist, addressed mutuality. He said, "There is complete symmetry in the distribution of assertion and dispute, revelation and concealment, prescription and conformity, among the partners of communication. As long as these symmetries exist, communication will not be hindered by constraints arising from its own structure."

In mutuality there is reciprocity. As individuals experience varying points of view as well as their own perspectives, a process of exploration, curiosity, and creativity unfurls. It's a mutual sharing of minds, hearts, and consciousness.

Theologian Martin Buber, in his book "I and Thou," refers to this quality of mutuality as an I-thou relationship where authenticity, inclusion, and mutual respect are present. Relationship building and mutuality go hand in hand. For mutuality to occur, there must be genuine interest in learning about another person's experiences. Mutuality is key to healthy and productive relationships. Here are some ways to establish mutuality:

> *Start early.* In the early stages of dialogue, share who you are and where you're coming from so others model your behavior. Be the first to step into this vulnerable territory.

> *Look for connection.* Topics will emerge that connect you to others. You will receive questions. Answer them honestly. You will establish bonds by listening and sharing. Basic dialogue will then transition into deeper, more meaningful dialogue.

> *Think beyond the book.* Dialogue is a process of creating solutions that can't be found in a book. You're leading an ongoing conversation that allows people to create meaning together. It's far from a chat. It's a form of mutual creation.

> *Value interpersonal relationships.* Mutuality leads to enhanced relationships. Regardless of the initial objectives for dialogue, almost invariably it results in effective interpersonal relationships. A dialogue that begins on the topic of

profitability can quickly shift into dialogue about interpersonal relationships among employees. Why? The strength of interpersonal relationships are almost always linked to desired outcomes.

Many business leaders rise to executive ranks because of their keen technical expertise, though their interpersonal skills may be lacking. Ironically, the very individuals who manage people may not be particularly adept at interpersonal relationships. If you place yourself in this category, dialogue can be pivotal to your career development. By leading dialogue, you have a training ground for facilitating better relationships.

This technique worked for one of my clients, a self-proclaimed "ice queen" turned collaborator. She learned how trust, friendship, and support could lead to critical reflection. Consider her transformational story as you think about your own interpersonal skills.

As one of few female executives, I constantly felt the need to check my emotions. My male counterparts were extremely unemotional. Was I emotional? How did I measure up? I felt pressure to improve my performance, follow the company line, and stay within the boundaries. It was painfully constraining. As a result, I was aloof in dealing with people. The barriers were obvious. It's no surprise I earned the nickname "Ice Queen." My interpersonal relationships were poor. People perceived me as cold.

I was on a spiritual path that made me realize I was no different than everyone else. I began to think of my job as a role. It was my responsibility to see the spark of the divine in others and myself. Things shifted the day I changed my perspective. Instead of focusing on others or defending myself, I opened up and looked for the divine in them. It worked. As I passed the janitor I said, "Hi, how are you?" Taken by surprise, he brightened and returned my genuine greeting. I did this with everyone I encountered. The results were incredible. I realized that true collaboration required genuine encounters. I had to recognize people for who they really were. We were all in it together. When I stopped holding myself apart from the system and became part of it, I was able to get real and collaborate. I had a transformative conversation with myself and discovered the power of mutuality. If people act authentically and see the genuineness in others, great things happen.

When a leader encourages mutual relationships, trust, friendship, and support will have an important impact on new learning and facilitate the way for critical reflection and authentic dialogue.

The power of not knowing

Some leaders are tempted to think they must know everything about everything, so to speak. As leaders gain professional maturity, they realize that's impossible and impractical. It's a leader's role to be the catalyst for others to become experts in their disciplines. This is why the best leaders are not necessarily specialists in their fields. They focus less on giving advice and more on asking probing questions. This technique allows employees to discover the best path on their own. That is the power of not knowing. To facilitate transformative conversations, a leader must "not know."

This practice is not as easy as it sounds, as evidenced through the reflections I've gathered in my research. Here's an example from a leader who trained herself to use a coaching approach.

There's a challenge in not blurting out "I know what this is about and where it's going." It's my role to help others recognize what may be obstructing them from forward progress. I used to be quick to give advice. I now realize advice closes dialogue. To be effective and nurture dialogue, I use a coaching approach and let others take ownership. The results are much better. People know what they should and shouldn't do, and they don't like to hear it reverberated back to them. If I discuss the possible outcome of their actions and the change they want to see, it's a totally different conversation.

Now consider this story. It's from a coach who helps clients clarify priorities. This illustrates how a position of not knowing can open up dialogue and bring unexpected results.

> An artist I work with is from New Orleans and the mother of two teenagers. I'll call her Gina. She left her husband, moved West, and opened a gallery. Gina is the kind of woman you would love to have on your committee. She quickly found herself receiving invitations to participate in organizations and events. This busy woman was raising two kids, trying to run a business, and create her own art at the same time. She craved down time to paint and create, but she couldn't find it. I asked, "What can you do to keep your priorities in mind, rather than accept every invitation you receive?" In my mind, I had the answer. Sticky notes. Gina needed to write "JUST SAY NO" on notes and post them on her pillow, mirror, phone, desk, purse. Everywhere. I didn't share my answer with her, but it was so obvious to me. I was certain that was her solution.
>
> Gina thought for a moment and said, "I've got it!" I smiled and told myself to act surprised when she offered sticky notes as the solution. She proceeded to tell me about a stream behind her home in New Orleans. She would retreat there when she needed time to reflect. "Before we left New Orleans, I visited the stream and put some rocks in my pocket. I brought them with me. I'm going to put a stone in my pocket so I'm always reminded of my priorities." I was amazed. This definitely wasn't what I had in mind, but it was creative and effective. In that instance I realized the beauty of not knowing.

Academics have promoted this position of not knowing for therapists, but it's an equally valuable stance for leaders who want to facilitate dialogue. It requires a leader to resist asking questions from a position of pre-understanding. The leader must recognize that he doesn't always have access to privileged information and can never fully understand another person. The leader must be willing to let himself be informed, rather than inform. He must desire to constantly learn more about what has been said, and what was left unspoken.

When I left Cuba as a teenager, I learned to love not knowing. I was thrilled to leave the known for the unknown. I knew I hated the known. There I knew exactly where I was, who I had to be, and all of my restrictions. The world opened up as I made my way toward the unknown. Suddenly everything seemed possible. Similarly, in dialogue you leave the comfort of the known to explore the unknown. Not knowing requires a humble, patient, open perspective. You are the student, not the expert. Not knowing can:

- Fill dialogue with fresh wonder.
- Encourage deeper dialogue.
- Create meaningful connections.
- Take you in unforeseen directions.
- Surprise you with an unexpected destination.
- Awaken new perspectives.

To gain comfort in the realm of not knowing, you must trust in the process. As a leader, trust that not knowing has its own wisdom and value. Trust that exploring what you don't know will take you to better places. Trust that the open space that not knowing opens will foster change and innovation. Trust that not knowing can propel you toward a daring adventure with magnificent results.

A leader who knows it all does not need anyone. Consequently, that leader does not connect with others. That leader does not inspire. Or motivate. Or collaborate. When you take the stance of not knowing, you will begin down the path of connecting others and motivating them to achieve their objectives. Once you create an open dialogue and position yourself as not knowing what's best, the mindset will come naturally. The benefits and rewards will begin to emerge. When you don't know you:

- Ask more questions that invite people into dialogue.
- Open spaces for exploration.
- Invite collaboration.
- Co-create better outcomes.
- Welcome surprises.

- Listen, hear and understand better.
- Are humble enough to keep learning.
- Prevent conflict by releasing perceived truths.

Not knowing opens the space for wisdom to emerge.

Participation

In dialogue, we are in a constant state of participation with others, the surrounding world, and ourselves. We may think of participation as talking, but the capacity to listen is at the heart of an interactive dialogue. We must learn to listen to our listening, as we may not be aware of how we listen.

Listening is active and interactive, not passive. A good listener conveys a sense of appreciation, acceptance, and understanding. These listening skills make the speaker come alive, which sustains enthusiasm. Good listening requires learning how to be fully present. It's the practice of releasing personal agenda and past history, and calming the emotions to listen with intensity.

During a dialogue you can share, talk, present, and tell. The book *Engaging Communication in Conflict* goes deeper to identify the key qualities of a participatory dialogue:

- You speak to be understood, rather than to prevail.
- You speak for yourself, rather than to represent "others" or "people."
- You present your perspective, rather than criticize others.
- You demonstrate how your opinion is grounded in your unique experiences, rather than advocate for your position as truth.
- You recognize many points of view, rather than polarize just two.
- You express your doubts, rather than show blind adherence.
- You explore ideas, rather than speak the party line.
- You explore complexity, rather than oversimplify.

Participating in dialogue is personal, exploratory, unpredictable, and sometimes messy. It's experiential. It's revealing. It's an exploration into new points of view, and even new ways of looking at those concepts.

It's an opportunity for people to support their viewpoints with stories. Oftentimes it brings intriguing results.

For example, during one of my retreats the leadership team grappled with how their organization should look in the near future. I instructed them to paint a picture illustrating their vision. As they painted together, they explored values, dreams, possibilities, and their individual roles. The result was not a work of art, but a beautiful product of their participatory minds and hearts.

Using your own voice to participate can be challenging. In his book "The Heart Aroused," poet David Whyte says, "Courageous speech has always held us in awe." He suggests it does so because it reveals our inner lives. When we speak our voice, we reveal the truth within us, regardless of all outside influence.

Speaking with your own voice requires you to distinguish between the "I should" and "I ought to" feelings that bombard your brain. It's a process of bringing your deepest thoughts from your innermost core to the forefront. It requires courage and determination. You must believe your feelings are valid. You must assume responsibility for speaking your beliefs regardless of the risks.

Listening

Dialogue makes listening the centerpiece of the conversation. People take listening for granted, yet it is a difficult skill to master. It takes more than two ears to listen. Leaders often report listening as their greatest weakness. They are not alone. Research indicates that only about 7 percent of the world's population is good at listening. Leaders busy themselves with talking, directing, telling, and influencing. In the process, they forget how vital listening is to dialogue.

Why is it difficult to listen?

- Your mind wants to stroll.
- You think four times faster than people talk, which gives you time to rehearse responses.
- Your to-do list is growing.
- You are bored by people who dwell on irrelevant details and express weak ideas.

- Your preconceptions color what you hear.
- You think the speaker has nothing of value to contribute.
- You can't hear, either due to real noise, inner noise, or the speaker's volume.
- You have another preferred way of taking in information.

Effective leadership requires effective listening skills. Why then, is the career development landscape littered with seminars and books on speaking and writing, but not on listening? Why do leaders leave their listening skills to chance?

The Chinese symbol for "to listen" best exemplifies the complexity of the act of listening. It is both artful and wise.

To Listen

YOU

EAR

EYES

UNDIVIDED
ATTENTION

The Chinese characters which make up
the verb "to listen" tell us
something significant about this skill.

HEART

The elements of the symbol essentially read "When I am listening to you, I give you my ears, my eyes, my undivided attention, and my heart." It is the best definition for wholehearted listening. Wholehearted listening requires all of you: your body, your heart, your energy. Total presence is required to *become* the listener rather than to *do* the listening.

To listen wholeheartedly, you must:

- Put your ego aside.
- Strive to understand and give authentic responses.
- Uphold appreciation and respect for the speaker.
- Suspend judgments.

- Block internal and external distractions to become totally attentive.
- Look for connection points rather than agreement points.
- Listen for the meanings behind words.
- Engage your heart and your head.
- Genuinely want to understand.
- Open your heart and exhibit patience.
- Sit quietly and make the speaker's words your priority.

As you master these skills, you will earn the speaker's loyalty and best efforts. You may be surprised to find that listening becomes your single most powerful skill, for it is an act of respect. Listening and seeking to understand creates more receptivity for being heard later. It includes eye contact, quieting the mind's rebuttals, and listening for information and emotional content. It includes asking questions to clarify meaning. It includes identifying meanings that emerge.

True listening promotes cooperation because it assumes the other person has dignity and something to offer. Dialogue requires you to cultivate the capacity to listen, rather than simply impose meaning on what other people say. To listen deeply is to blend with someone to the point where you begin to participate fully in understanding how they understand. If you do not truly listen, you only have your own interpretation.

Listening together is an equally important skill. To listen together is to learn to be part of a larger whole, where the voice and meaning emerge from the group. Themes will surface through this shared experience. Do not be surprised when you begin to hear others voice your thoughts. As this occurs, the next steps will become obvious to everyone. This flow of meaning occurs when individuals relax their grip on what they think, and listen to what others think. This is dialogue emerging. This is what happens when you talk less and listen more.

I have never heard anyone complain of negative side effects from listening more. That suggests it is an excellent skill to add to your arsenal. Here are seven tips to help you listen up:

1. *Focus.* You focus on what you value most. When you pay attention to another person, you tell the person you value him or her.
2. *Just listen.* Don't think about what you are going to say. Understand the message.

3. *Establish a dialogue.* Confirm understanding by rephrasing pertinent points. Summarize what you hear. Then offer an opinion or fact. Your role is to help people think critically.

4. *Be curious.* Never assume you know what the other person is thinking or feeling. Ask intelligent questions. The speaker will feel valued.

5. *Respect silence.* When pauses occur in the flow of conversation, avoid the urge to fill the void. People need moments of silence to digest information.

6. *Remain patient.* It is rude to interrupt. It suggests you care most about your own opinion.

7. *Think first.* Wait a few seconds before you talk. Is your contribution relevant? Is it the right time? If not, keep quiet.

Responsible listening is an art form worth mastering. You can develop and strengthen it with practice. The result will be a sustainable competitive advantage over your peers and competitors.

Suspension

True dialogue requires suspending assumptions, judgment, and evaluation. Suspension means stopping assumptions from interfering with listening. You don't carry out assumptions or suppress them, or judge them as valid or invalid. It takes discipline to change directions, as you stop, step back, and see the situation with fresh eyes. To put it another way, you do not move into agreement or debate. Instead, you build bridges across the diversity of opinions, assumptions, backgrounds, and ideas.

When you suspend judgment, you learn to hold your opinions lightly. You consciously open yourself to hearing and understanding each person's point of view. This creates a space between your judgments and reactions. It allows you to hear the person in a new way. Rather than formulate your thoughts in advance, you allow the conversation to influence you. It takes practice to acknowledge and observe your thoughts without acting on them. As you observe what happens as it unfolds, you establish a climate of trust and safety in the group.

The word "suspend" comes from the Latin root *suspendere*, which means, "to hang below." In this sense, suspending is like stretching out a large canvas to reveal its intricacies to the world. It requires you to let what you know – or think you know – hang out in front of you. As you release assumptions and stereotypes, your mind can open to change. The unexpected can occur. Once you free yourself of habitual responses, you will feel fresh and alive in your dialogue.

Openness

An open mind breeds open thought. Flexible, humble individuals have open minds. They know they aren't always right. They stand their ground while being profoundly open to new ideas. As they express opinions, feelings, values, and ideas clearly, they listen openly to others.

As a leader, what can you learn when you are open? By listening with openness you may:

- Learn about the reasons for your beliefs.
- Better understand the positions and experiences of others.
- Discover important differences among people who agree on an issue.
- Realize that you share concerns among those with whom you disagree.
- Come to respect others participating in the dialogue.
- Gain awareness for the complexity of the issues.
- Have a stronger ability to live with ambiguity.
- Discover new ways to talk productively about the issue.
- See that former animosities and hostilities can be reduced.
- Find ways to work together despite your differences.

It is critical to open your mind and see the situation from other participants' perspectives. As a leader, opportunities abound to promote openness. You can advocate for openness in the tone of your emails, in the way you conduct meetings, and through the inspirational messages you deliver at companywide meetings. It takes discipline to park your ego at the door and remain open to hear and seek input. As you encourage openness in dialogue, you will reap the reward of harvesting diverse thoughts to further progress.

Meaning making

We are meaning-making machines. Our brains and hearts are programmed to find meaning. When we don't find it we feel empty, unhappy, and devoid of purpose. When we do we are joyful and fulfilled in work and life.

Successful leaders understand that it's their role to make sense of what people do together. Leaders make meaning. They communicate meaning through their words, the images and stories they share, and by recognizing employees who exemplify organizational values.

Jack Mezirow, who created the theory of transformative learning, defines learning as "the process of using a prior interpretation to construe a new or revised interpretation of the meaning of one's experience as a guide to future action." In his view, dialogue helps transform our taken-for-granted frames of reference to make them more inclusive, discriminating, open, and reflective. In this way we can generate new beliefs and opinions that will prove more true or justified to guide action for change.

Mezirow promotes a constructivist perspective of reality, meaning reality is more subjective than objective. Therefore, people construct meaning through the lens of their past experiences. Meaning is built in relation with others. As people analyze and pose questions, they make meaning through dialogue. They convert their long-held frames of reference through transformative learning, and become capable of generating new beliefs to guide their actions.

As a leader, you may recognize hidden meanings that live just under the surface of shared experiences. How do these meanings inform and shape dialogue? Do these underlying beliefs, values, and emotions influence individual meaning making? How do they impact the group's ability to construct new meanings?

As you help bring hidden meanings to the surface, your team members will make connections. This effort will help them make meaning, and strengthen your personal meaning making. When people express their values in the relational aspect of dialogue, meaning creates community.

Reflection

Dialogue constantly invites people to reflect on their thoughts and actions. Then it prompts them to reflect on their reflections. Finally, it begs them to reflect on their reflections about their reflections. While it's a cumbersome thought, this process is collaborative. Just as ocean waves have a rhythm – back and forth, calmly in and out, churning, exploding, constantly interacting with the shoreline – so do reflections.

Reflection encourages people to explore their values and the meaning of those values. It compels individuals to examine alternative ways of acting and reacting. It can help leaders learn from mistakes, reconsider options, and think about the big picture. It all happens in the context of dialogue, both inner dialogue and dialogue with others.

Critical reflection is the key to transformative learning. This kind of reflection occurs after people validate their emotions. Through this process people challenge the validity of stereotypes and prior learning. The process of reflection in dialogue is conducive to double- and triple-loop learning since it encourages single-, double-, and triple-loop feedback.

- In *single-loop feedback*, you learn that your actions do not achieve a pre-established goal. As you adjust your actions, you increase the possibility of achieving the goal. This kind of feedback is simply a change in behavior to a specific situation.

- In *double-loop feedback*, you learn that the structure of the person or system is problematic. Flaws reveal themselves in your meaning-making system. You learn by examining alternative policies and objectives from new perspectives, rather than improving the functionality of existing perspectives. You develop a capacity for integrative awareness and use feedback to alter your strategies for gaining understanding. It is deeper than behavioral change.

- In *triple-loop feedback*, you learn through awareness and reflection. You evaluate multiple levels of complexities, paradoxes, and polarities present in a situation. You review initial conditions, environmental variables, personal responses, strategies, tactics, and behaviors. You critique results. Rather than abandon a vision, you inquire in an open way. You analyze assumptions, fixed patterns, beliefs, and habits. You are willing to change your vision, strategies, and actions. The feedback you receive might lead to a change in context. It might disrupt the organizational culture. This will potentially lead to deep transformation.

Here's how my research participants perceived dialogue as a way to invite reflection and encourage transformation:

Dialogue uses advanced communication skills. It goes far beyond the elementary level of communication. It is not a monologue. It invites people to reflect. They ask themselves questions that make them think. Evolve.

Leaders who use a collaborative, reflective approach create more memorable and meaningful experiences. They ask probing and open-ended questions: "What do you think about this idea? How does this situation make you feel?" These questions encourage people to reflect on their reflections. It creates a continuous conversation.

Dialogue permits people to wonder. They see a riddle as a positive thing because it leads them to critical reflection. Transformative dialogue is about learning from experiences and reflecting on them. It leads to making decisions and taking action.

By reflecting together and asking key questions, you drill down to core issues. Those issues are often contrary to what exists on the surface. If someone says they hate their boss, further dialogue will likely reveal the core issue. Perhaps the employee really feels her skills aren't sharp enough to compete. The reflective process helps people move beyond their presentation of issues to real issues. It promotes fundamental change.

These examples underscore the power and importance of dialogue. Critical change can begin when one individual reflects. As a leader who understands and uses dialogue to listen and share, you will see the benefits spread throughout your team.

Possibility

Some organizations train employees to think and ask, "What's wrong?" Many leaders encourage their teams to ponder, "How can we fix it?" This is demoralizing, yet typical. Shift the conversation to a dialogue focused on possibilities. You can do this by asking these two questions:

> *What's possible?* This question invites unprecedented creativity. Take for example the leader of a nonprofit organization searching for an incubator to send to a third-world country orphanage. If the first hospital representative she calls declines her request, she can take the conversation to the next level. She may ask about other possible donations, and secure valuable medical equipment in the process.

> *Who cares?* Use this question to discover people with shared passions. It's how you create a tribe, or a group of people who share the same passion for an issue. The situation will deteriorate unless people who care surround you. Caring involves raising the bar to the point where the team must stretch. For example, maybe you've stayed at a hotel where the front desk staff won't pick up the phone when you call. If your shower curtain bar is falling away from the wall, you need someone to fix it. Yet, no one seems to care. When you finally track down the manager, he tells you times are tough, money is tight, and that he inherited the front desk staff from the previous manager. Caring is a competitive advantage. Make it a point to care, and surround yourself with others who share in that philosophy.

Inquiry

Powerful questions contain the seeds from which dialogue can grow. For this reason, it's important to ask significant questions. Powerful answers grow from powerful questions. Inquiry comes from genuine curiosity, and can help people reflect, gain clarity, explore possibilities, and recall forgotten competencies and resources. As people respond to questions, they can entertain options and begin to view things differently. You may be surprised by the answers you receive when you ask questions.

Be aware that unproductive questioning may shut people down. They include:

- Rhetorical questions to make a point.
- Interrogative questions to uncover hidden information.
- Critical questions to point out flaws in the person's arguments.

In dialogue, it's best to ask open and nonjudgmental questions designed to learn more. Strive to discover together. It's a place to put challenges on the table in search of innovative solutions. Look more for meaning, and less for absolute truths. This process can foster innovation.

Curiosity and inquiry are the cornerstones of learning. Transformational learning emphasizes critical reflection. When you ask questions out of curiosity, they will reveal solutions and perspectives that may not have otherwise surfaced. Be sincere and ask questions because you truly want to know. In the process of explaining, people will come to better understanding. If you ask the right questions, people will provide the right answers. Dialogue is especially productive when you use different kinds of questions:

Open questions

Ask open questions to stimulate creativity and bring important connections and relationships to mind. Open questions reveal new avenues of thought, stimulate creativity, and help bring important connections and relationships to mind. Listen with respect. When others feel you're taking their comments seriously they'll share more and learn more about themselves in the process.

> *Try this technique*: Pair people with conversation partners. Instruct them to share something about their personal or professional lives. The listener can only respond with curious questions designed to learn more. The listener can't agree, disagree, commiserate, argue, give advice, or tell a story. It may be difficult for the listener, but it will lead to sharing and new learning.

Story questions

In asking story questions, your goal is to elicit more details about the story. As you listen, you'll hear details that will prompt you to ask further probing questions. As the layers of the story unfold, there will be a more profound sharing experience. This provides a great opportunity for exploring various points of view.

> *Try this technique*: Pair people with conversation partners. Instruct them to share a story about an experience that was special to them. The listener can only ask story questions to gain further insight into the story. Let participants see how deeply they can delve into the story, and then switch roles.

Systemic questions

Systemic questions are designed to help participants expand the conversation and talk about relationships. It forces a shift from the individualistic mindset to the systemic one. Systemic questions encourage thinking about connections, new possibilities, and comparisons. They often illustrate the link between statements and behaviors. Most importantly, systemic questions remind participants that their thoughts, actions, and statements are connected to others' thoughts and actions.

> *Try this technique*: Instead of asking your manager why her meetings are unproductive, ask, "What would you need to change for your meetings to become more productive?" Then follow up with, "If your meetings were more productive, how would things be different in your organization?" Your systemic question will open her mind to new possibilities. Her responses may lead you to ask, "You are saying you're surprised by your team's immature behavior. How can you tell when they're being immature? What surprises you most about this?" Posing questions in this manner can help the person explore new patterns of interaction to improve results.

Inquiry is a vehicle for exploration, reflection, and learning. Questions invite people to talk *with* each other, not *at* each other. When you assume a not-knowing stance and ask questions from a place of curiosity, you stimulate the other's subjectivity and creativity. You help expand the conversation.

Positive

A transformative dialogue focuses on strengths to build a foundation of personal confidence that facilitates a deeper exploration of issues. At least 80 percent of those I interviewed for my doctoral research said they wanted others to explore concepts from a position of strength rather than from a place of brokenness. These summaries highlight the significant results that can be realized through positive behavior:

> I focus on strengths when I begin a dialogue. I ask the person to talk about his good qualities, what he can do, how he impacts people, and what draws people to him. This helps me follow-up with a positive comment that I pull from his reflection. Most leaders don't receive positive feedback. By saying, "One thing I see that makes you a great leader is your ability to ..." I provide courage so that person can look deeper inside. This technique helps celebrate who they are and what they have become.

> One of the best leaders I have ever worked with wasn't aware of key things he was doing in the emotional intelligence arena until I told him. I gave him an article to read and told him, "Here are some of the things you are doing. I don't know if anyone ever showed you this. This is what good leaders do, and you are doing them." He said his peers would criticize him for doing some of the very things the article mentioned. It was the perfect opportunity to remind him that he was getting better results than his peers. He sat up and said, "Wow!" Leaders just aren't used to receiving positive feedback.

> My client, new to his challenging leadership role, wanted to improve his team's performance. After working with him

for nearly a year, he said everyone on his team was so dedicated and willing to cooperate that he wondered if he was making it too easy. Productivity was up, clients were happy, deadlines were met, and conflicts had diminished. Why was he uneasy? It hit me. He still carried the mindset that work should be painful. Regardless of the positive outcomes he was experiencing as a result of his positive behavior, he feared being perceived as soft.

As the individuals in these examples focused on the positive, they elicited change. This is consistent with newer trends and research being done in the fields of appreciative inquiry, appreciative leadership and positive psychology. Research shows that people respond better to positive comments and approaches. Focusing on what works, rather than what's broken, is a more effective way to learn, grow, innovate, and create enduring positive change. Imagine the positive dialogue that might result if you open your next meeting by asking, "Who has good news to share?"

Researchers David Cooperrider and Suresh Srivastva conceived the concept of appreciative inquiry. Its underlying principle is that positive images lead to positive actions. Appreciative inquiry improves performance and promotes transformation by encouraging people to study, discuss, learn from, and build on what is working, rather than try to fix problems. It naturally removes resistance to change and promotes transformation, even though critics have raised questions about its effectiveness.

In "Positive Leadership: Strategies for Extraordinary Performance," author Kim Cameron discusses a study that highlights the benefits of positivity. Results showed that in high-performing organizations, top managers used abundant positive comments. A ratio between 5-9 positive statements to every negative statement was predictive of the highest levels of performance. Similar studies uphold the power of positive words.

You can become a positive force both in dialogue and daily life when you lift others. These five strategies are designed to help you influence others with positive words for positive results.

1. *Be positive.* Your words reflect your thoughts. You can't give positive feedback if you have a negative attitude. Cultivate a positive

outlook by looking for the good in people in situations. Share positive thoughts, feedback, and encouragement.

2. *Screen.* American author and motivational speaker Zig Ziglar said, "You are what you are because of what goes into your mind." Don't let gloomy people and bad news infect you. Filter out the negative.

3. *Begin the day with a dose of positive input.* Just as a nutritional breakfast is best for your body, inspiring and uplifting news is best for your mind. Kick off the day with the positive.

4. *Lift others with your words.* Choose to replace hurtful words with those that encourage, engage, and enrich others. You can choose to complain or express appreciation. Tear people down or build them up. Ignore people or greet them. Demand or request. Be rude or kind. Make conscious word choices.

5. *Encourage and affirm others.* Instead of focusing on people's mistakes, emphasize what they did right. Praising employees for their achievements will positively impact them and the organization. Sincere and specific acknowledgment stimulates people to think and create greater things.

Humor

Humor and positivity go hand in hand. You can use lighthearted, non-offensive humor to facilitate dialogue and bring perspective to difficult situations. It also encourages learning and fosters positive relationships. Well-placed humor can turn negative situations into positive ones. Consider the following reflections from my research:

> I rely on humor because I like to laugh with my team. That said, there is a time for humor, but it can't come at the expense of others. Humor lets me ask something that is pretty far forward, and my team can treat it as a seed.

> People learn best in an atmosphere of play. Dialogue is not all play, but it includes playful interaction. I want people to feel positive and like themselves. I like to think they will leave with more of a smile on their faces, as well as a sense of having learned something. A little discomfort is inevitable,

but the pleasure of humor helps participants overcome pain. There needs to be more pleasure than pain.

> An executive I was working with called me in a frenzied state. He had no idea how he was going to get his task done, considering his competing deadlines. I said, "It sounds like we have a disaster here. Let's add some perspective. If you don't get this done, will the world really come to an end? Will your department be deleted? Will the company go bankrupt?" The executive's worry turned to laughter and relief. Bring light to dark situations. It's more productive than telling someone to stop hyperventilating, because they'll push back, retort and respond with, "Yes, but…"

Using humor includes seeing the best in others. If you train yourself to think in these terms, you will quickly begin to see the good in people and situations. Leaders use power and influence in many different ways, resulting in a variety of outcomes. Some attempt to influence others through threats and criticism. People respond to negativity with fear. Other leaders move people harmoniously toward exceptional results through positivity and humor. Positive influence is undoubtedly more desirable, leaves less damage, and gets better results.

Why is it important to create a positive culture?

Many years ago the wise Dale Carnegie wrote, "Any fool can criticize, condemn and complain – and most fools do." You are no fool. You can train yourself to look for the good in yourself, your world and others. By focusing on positives and using humor, you can help people become creative, innovative, and collaborative. Here's why it's important to be positive:

> *Higher performance*: A positive culture yields higher performance and better marketplace position.

> *More effective change initiatives*: Employees in positive work environments are more receptive to change. They're prone to adapt and seek challenges.

71

Higher productivity and talent retention: A positive corporate culture creates more engaged and satisfied workers. Happier workers result in higher productivity.

More successful mergers: Organizations with positive cultures are more likely to have successful mergers. It may; however, be difficult to blend two corporate cultures into a unified culture. Post merger, it may be best to establish a new positive culture.

Better talent management: Successful hiring, retention and training are significantly associated with positive corporate cultures.

To successfully facilitate dialogue, first examine your own integrity. Are your beliefs and personal attributes congruent with what you convey? Do you share from your heart? Do you practice confidentiality? Are you non-judgmental? As you put others at ease, you will create a space of calmness and trust. This setting compels people to reflect. When you allow others to speak without interruption and ask curious questions, you will make meaning together. Chemistry will emerge and dialogue will begin to flow easily. Your relationships will turn into alliances, offering untold possibilities for change and growth. When you enable such positive synergy, you'll be in high demand and go far in your career.

4   *Harvesting Knowledge to Create Action*

I HEAR IT TIME AND AGAIN: conversations can be easily forgotten, distorted or lost. People fear that no action will emerge from dialogue, or that discoveries will be difficult to implement. They're valid concerns. That's why it's critical to harvest and share the wisdom that results from dialogue.

Nurturing productive conversations is a fundamental leadership skill. It's necessary when the goal is transformative change. Leaders can hone their skills to facilitate strategic conversations that stimulate deep learning, forward movement, and transformation. To be fully understood, it must be experienced.

It was spring. I was meeting with a group of 30 executives from five different management teams across the United States. Prior to a global acquisition four years earlier, they had represented five smaller companies. This was their first meeting as a group. My task: facilitate a process to help them find common goals for the USA group and teach them how to nurture transformative conversation. They also wanted to build trust within their circle. I had one-and-a-half days.

Day 1

We did several exercises using a variety of dialogue styles. There was circle work. Small group work. Open-space work. One-on-one interactions. My visual recorder helped capture the conversations by drawing in a visual and meaningful way. Several things were obvious by the end of the first day:

- The leaders were confused about their identity.
- They were unsure of what corporate name to use.
- They felt disempowered in relation to what their European leadership wanted, and what they perceived as different needs in the United States.
- They were waiting for someone to fix the issue.

Day 2

I knew it was critical for these executives to gain awareness of their strength and power as a united group. We began the day with two minutes of silence. They were to look within to explore the personal strengths they were willing to bring into the room and their organization. Then I asked them to stand, circulate, and share three of their strengths with as many people as possible in two minutes of interaction. To harvest those strengths, I had them return to the large circle and share what they heard among their colleagues.

The feedback included good listener, problem solver, loyal, integrity, playful, good humor, balance, bridge builder, passion and caring, among others. This led to a discussion on the strengths they cherished from their former small companies – things they didn't want to lose. They jotted those strengths on sticky notes and grouped them by theme in the front of the room. Two surprises emerged:

1. The strengths they wanted to transfer from their small companies to the larger organization were similar.
2. Their sentiments aligned with the values the new organization was trying to promote. They were just worded differently.

The energy in the room shifted. The leaders were now united in purpose. They had optimism. They were willing to take responsibility and make big things happen. They spent the rest of the morning making action plans for four key areas. Their accomplishments were impressive.

More importantly, they left feeling aligned as one team, not five individual teams. During their final reflections they reported feeling free and secure, that they had lived their values and that they were leaving as one team. These leaders experienced a great dialogue that resulted in concrete action points. They left with a visual recording of their conversations so they could easily share what transpired.

This is just one example of how dialogue can transform a group. It never fails to bring hope, optimism, positive energy, and empowerment for change.

Ideas for documenting collective knowledge

It is difficult to describe a dialogue. The dialogue can be quickly lost and forgotten unless there is a method in place to collect the experience. Visual records and pictures work exceptionally well. They're colorful, understandable and story based. They're memorable. Sometimes these visual records even find a place of permanence in PowerPoint presentations or framed in conference rooms. In these instances, the dialogue lives on as the conversation continues. Visuals can also be used as reminders for follow-up action and implementation.

Participants in world cafés, conferences, open-space technologies, dialogue circles, and other forms of conversation use innovative ways to capture the essence of their dialogues. Here are just a few ideas:

Make headlines

At the close of a session, invite the group to create and publish a newspaper with the day's headlines and a summary of the collective dialogue. A volunteer can be the chief editor. This will help participants build from a base as they have further conversations and make action plans.

Create idea cards

Within a small group, people can turn in cards indicating the ideas that impressed them the most. Post the cards and cluster related cards into a large poster.

Multiplying partnerships

Ask people to share their new knowledge with a partner. Encourage them to link up with another pair, and then those four with four more. It's fun, and each linking layer encourages people to speak with more brevity and focus on more important themes. It's an active way for people to get a snapshot of the collective wisdom emerging from the dialogue.

Record and reflect

Using easel-size sheets, have people at each table record the words and graphics that represent their ideas and understandings. They can share the recording with the larger group, or tour tables to get a taste for other conversations. At the conclusion, someone can gather the papers, take snapshots of the notes, and share the collective record with everyone.

Create an exhibit

After a day of dialogue, divide people into groups and ask each to draw a picture of their gains from the day. Post the pictures on a big sheet of paper or on the walls to form an exhibit. When everyone gathers at the gallery to talk about each group's creation, encourage questions and insights. Add any additional comments. It can become a growing picture of the dialogue.

Write a story

Facilitate a story-writing exercise and encourage participants to depict the dialogue that has unfolded. It can be a mythical story, fable, or nonfiction work.

Have a poetry contest

Challenge each group to capture the day's dialogue in an original poem. This exercise may bring out humor, and it will definitely be memorable.

Perform a skit

The imagination knows no limit, and some groups may benefit greatly from creating a skit or video. They can set it to music, or mime in silence. There are many creative ways to summarize and share experiences using a variety of mediums.

Use a graphic recorder

This is a wonderful tool to help the group – especially a large one – understand conversation as it unfolds. Employ a visual specialist to record people's reflections and dialogue in words and pictures on wall murals. Rolling blackboards work too. Participants see the dialogue as it emerges and have a visual record that helps them understand and share the big picture. People easily identify different threads and see how key ideas connect, which in turn leads to systemic thinking.

Connect the dots

Following a dialogue, distribute index cards and ask, "What question can we explore further to help you move forward in your role?" Group the answers on the index cards by obvious themes. Write the overarching questions on a large canvas. Then distribute four sticky dots, with one containing an "X" and the remainders in different colors. Instruct participants to place their "X" on the question that needs the most exploration. They can use their other dots to rank topics accordingly. A visual map will emerge, creating the next day's agenda.

Regardless of the technique you use to document collective knowledge, it's important to allow a few moments of silence. This encourages the group to reflect. They can center their thoughts and jot down their ideas. This frees them to listen more intently to others. By shifting attention from the individual to the process of dialogue and the big picture that emerges, they can better understand key facets of their conversations and see meaning emerge.

From dialogue to effective action

Many leaders keep their foot on the gas. They go full throttle and live in a world of non-stop action. There's no time to slow down. There are big goals to achieve and tight deadlines to meet. Dialogue? There's no time for such fluff!

Leaders in the fast lane should be very careful. Unless they yield to curves and danger zones, they may soon find themselves in a major wreck. Their fast-paced tendencies create unnecessary stress. They blur out valuable opportunities for reflection, awareness, and learning. Transformative learning and change require time for reflection and convening. Leaders who create time to slow down, unplug a bit, and assess their status will be shocked at the results. They may adopt new perspectives and welcome dialogue into their lives.

As a leader who wants effective action and change to occur, abandon the faster-is-better mentality for a moment. Instead encourage:

- Listening
- Open dialogue
- Presentation and discussion of options
- Multiple viewpoints
- Process reviews
- Critical evaluation

The next time you feel your adrenalin surge, remember that slow *is* fast. For fast action, start slowly. It is counterintuitive, and it is effective. It's understandable that you want action and you want it now. You talk about it. Share it in your strategic plan. Discuss it with the media. Perhaps you spearhead a change campaign. Share dazzling presentations with your direct reports. Push. Rally. Advocate for action. And nothing happens.

If you find yourself in this cycle, try plugging dialogue into the equation. There's no better way to explain how dialogue leads to relationship building than through this powerful example from the three-day meeting I facilitated in Iceland. The goal: bring together an international group of 60 people who had been working together for two years in a recently designed section of the company. As you read this synopsis, notice how the seemingly slow start contributed to growth.

> The group hoped to unify criteria and push innovation forward. They likewise desired increased worldwide collaboration. After two years of failed attempts, they realized the value in coming together for face-to-face relationship building. However, they did not want to lose time in unnecessary talk. They spent the first morning getting to know each other through activities and mixed-group conversation. We

discussed greetings, circles, and dialogue. People had time to greet one another and share stories of strength. We gave the lead team an opportunity to discuss their struggles. We reflected and took turns talking in a large circle, interacting in smaller groups, and reconvening for reflection.

Their feedback was both encouraging and uplifting. In summary:

- They thought the process would be difficult, but they actually enjoyed it.
- They learned more about each other as a result of the exercise.
- There was collective anxiety, and people were relieved to learn "it's not just me."
- It's easier to feel close to people when you share interests and backgrounds.
- You can learn a lot about another person in a very brief period of time.

What emerged highlighted the importance and power of greeting, stories, circles, systems, and diversity. The profound nature of these elements of dialogue cannot be overemphasized. Does your leadership style include or exclude these connecting techniques? Reflect as you read through their features and benefits.

The power of greeting

A greeting is a first impression. Its quality sets the tone for the rest of the interaction. People in the Western world tend to offer superficial greetings like "Hi" or "What's up?" or "How are you?" They tend to elicit generic reactions. Leaders can use greetings to their advantage if they recognize the greeting as a gift to be used wisely. People make their presence known to others through greetings. These exchanges can be thin and meaningless, or they can enrich relationships.

I first thought seriously about greetings after hearing the daughter of a Holocaust survivor explain how her mother retained her humanity during a very inhumane time. To survive – and remember she was a human – she continuously reminded herself that human connection was possible. Each day, she would purposefully take a moment to look a fellow inmate in the eyes and give the Hebrew greeting "Shalom Uveracha," which roughly translates as "peace and blessing." It gave her hope to receive just an instant of acknowledgement, of shared humanity. It kept her alive. Her simple greeting connected her to others. She gave a gift and received one in return.

Greeting is a gift of connection

The Zulu people in South Africa understand the gift of greeting. There is great depth of meaning in their greeting "Sawun bona" or *I see you*. The greeting begins as two people look deep into each other's eyes. They establish a deep human connection without any words. Eye contact is akin to soul contact. This sense of oneness inspires better communication.

Babies intuitively know how to use their eyes to communicate. They look to their parents' eyes for affirmation, love, and understanding when they are too young to express themselves verbally. Young children also know that they must make eye contact with their parents to get the attention they crave. They're not satisfied when their calls for attention are met with a perfunctory word or remark. They demand full eye-to-eye contact. They'll climb into a lap and say, "Look at me!" if that's what it takes to get it.

Why does eye contact form such meaningful connections? It immediately puts human beings on a level playing field because it's a form of simultaneous communication. Eye contact does not require turn taking, as in talking. Looking deeply into another's eyes is synonymous with giving the gift of equality.

Greeting is a gift of affirmation

According to the Zulu tradition, to say, "I see you" offers an intention to release any preconceptions and judgments so that, "I can see you as God created you." To hear, "I see you" is an affirmation that you exist, that you are both equal and that mutual respect is present. This tradition highlights the importance of affirming others' presence. By fully acknowledging another person, we affirm them and energize our relationship with them. It validates both individuals' humanity.

How does this Zulu tradition translate to your role as a leader? For you, there may be nothing more rewarding than seeing a team member light up while receiving recognition of his humanity and greatness. There are many ways for you to tell your team members "I see you."

- When you focus on another person and look into his eyes, you say *I SEE YOU.*
- When you pause and give full attention to the person in front of you, you say *I SEE YOU.*
- When you acknowledge another person's presence, you say *I SEE YOU.*
- When you give a compliment, you say *I SEE YOU.*
- When you share an empowering message, you say *I SEE YOU.*
- When you notice someone's strengths, you say *I SEE YOU.*
- When you recognize a contribution, you say *I SEE YOU.*

Greeting is a gift of attention

The response to the Zulu greeting is "Sikhona" or *I am here.* "I am here" declares the receiver's intent to be fully present in the moment. It signals a willingness to engage with integrity. It gives the promise of full presence and suggests, "This is the real me and I will be honest and speak my truth."

As people become more globally connected through technology, they seem to crave more attention. They are starved for human interaction. It has become a novelty to actually see – in the flesh – the person on the other end. When there is a real face-to-face interaction, it's common for one of the people to break the attention for a quick text check. In this sense, giving complete and undivided attention has become a priceless gift.

"I am here" demonstrates the willingness to give the gift of proximity, community, and companionship. The connection that results from sharing in the present is the real indicator of healthy relationships. For these reasons, it's important to resist the urge to rush through greetings. Recognize the importance of presence and validation in your everyday encounters, both formal and casual. Your words of greeting can energize or deflect relationships. Practice acknowledging those you meet, and exit each human exchange satisfied knowing you brought someone else into existence by acknowledging his or her humanity.

The power of story

Storytelling is a powerful way to discover who we are, what we know, and how we grow. It lets us evaluate the factors that make us strong, and those that contribute to our growth. What's in a story?

Stories:

- Are powerful.
- Allow us to connect and know each other as individuals.
- Can rally an organization around a dream of a better future.
- Capture attention.
- Remind people of their roots.
- Energize people to take action.
- Focus the collective mind on solutions.
- Inspire and motivate.
- Can be powerful tools to change organizations.
- Are effective for communicating almost anything.

How can the simple act of storytelling bring so many benefits? Why have stories been used and passed down throughout the ages to offer wisdom? Consider these reasons:

> *Stories are natural and easy.* Humans seem to have an ability to tell and follow a story from a very early age. Listening to stories is refreshing and energizing. When it's time to share stories, the energy in the room becomes palpable. The storyteller invites the listener to visualize a different world. The shared imagining between teller and listener creates a common space where change becomes desirable.

> *Stories help people cope with the complex.* Stories provide a simple way to communicate complexity. Organizations and the changes needed within them can be tedious and complicated. People can more easily understand and make sense of change by sharing stories.

Stories bypass resistance. The mind doesn't critique stories. It follows them. Listeners don't analyze the story. They live it. The mindset is fundamentally different, more collaborative than critical.

Stories engage feelings. By triggering emotions, stories offer deep meaning. People need to see and feel before change can occur. Emotions can help or hinder change. Change leaders who tell stories make their points in emotionally engaging ways.

Tell stories to elicit transformative change. Tell stories of how you arrived at your vision. Tell stories about successful changes occurring in the organization. Tell stories about creative and innovative individuals. Tell stories about the future. Rely on storytelling as one of your most useful strategies for achieving successful transformation.

The power of circles

The circle is an ancient form of meeting. It has brought people together in respectful conversation for thousands of years. The circle has served as the foundation for many cultures. It's the natural format for sitting down and building relationships. It begs participants to have receptive attitudes, speak thoughtfully, and listen intently. The circle is the ideal shape for listening, being heard, earning respect, thinking, and creating together.

Sitting in rows, as in the case of classrooms, auditoriums, churches, and planes, is a deviation from the long-established circle. Looking at the back of other people's heads creates discomfort. It's disconnected. In the business world, as teams sit along the straight edges of tables and desks, they struggle to find ways to reach out and connect. This format fosters more separation than connection.

Transformative conversations occur in circles. When people assemble chairs into a ring, it seems to make the experiences bigger, the reflections more intense, and the dialogue wiser. This is part of dialogue's seductive nature. It sparks an energy that can clarify issues within the group. It helps transform the group.

The power of systems

For a long time, organizational leaders thought and spoke in mechanistic and linear terms. That was ideal for getting standardized things done in a society dominated by manufacturing and machines. As companies began to shift their focus from widgets to ideas, leaders began to think organically. The organization became a living system.

Living systems function together, just like groups function to generate ideas and solve problems. In dialogue, the system is formed as large or small groups work together to find solutions, and to create together what is and what will be. It gives attention to what emerges in the present.

You can apply the power of systems by dividing the large group into working groups of four or five people, and then tasking the groups to explore a question or concept, or to develop a vision. Encourage each participant to keepthese basic questions in mind:

- Where is your attention directed?
- What's at the heart of the conversation?
- What is the focused intent?

Ask each group to assign a table host. The host's job is to pay special attention to the conversation and make sure everyone contributes by keeping some kind of visual record on the sheets of paper at the table. After 15 minutes, ask everyone except the host to move and choose a different table to continue the conversation. You can do two or three rounds of conversation. Choose a different host for each round so everyone has the opportunity to circulate. As the conversation flows and shifts, it will be amazing to observe the system change dynamics and become more unified.

In dialogue, all parts of the system play a role in developing the process, content, and solutions. Everyone has a hand in developing the other participants. Just like living systems can't be totally controlled, the perceptions and reactions of the dialoguing system can't be controlled. They develop through conversation. Individuals' perceptions change as the system functions, learns, and grows together.

The power of diversity

Diversity has to do with differences in how people see, categorize, and go about understanding, describing, and improving their world. It's influenced by the diversity in the identity of people: their country, culture, ethnicity, social status, and family. It is particularly driven by personal cognitive preferences in processing information. Diversity of thought is vital for the good of the system.

Understanding, leveraging, and welcoming the diversity of people's minds is critical to success. Look for your team's strengths and areas that need development. Strive to build greater tolerance and respect for the unique strengths of each person. Be inclusive of everyone's thoughts. Differences add to the collective benefit. Invite people to collaborate. Minds that work together bond and succeed together.

People have a tendency to distrust those of other cultures and ethnicities before interacting with them. They may think, "If you are not like me, you are suspect and I can't trust you." However, if there is enough opportunity for interaction, trust develops through understanding. You can learn to appreciate differences, and so can everyone else. The power of diversity can strengthen organizational culture.

Smart leaders surround themselves with people who offer various strengths and ways to perceive and process information. You can avoid groupthink by encouraging a free-flowing dialogue where diverse thinking is appreciated. A diverse atmosphere encourages people to take concerted actions and make wiser decisions.

You can reach inclusive decisions through dialogue. As a result, collaboration and cooperation will occur in a compassionate, fair, just, and effective way. Thus, the resulting action will be more efficient.

Part II

Making Transformative Conversations Possible

Making Transformative Conversations Possible

THERE ARE NO HARD-AND-FAST RULES to ensure that dialogue works. Dialogue happens between people, and no one person controls it. Nevertheless, there are basic guidelines that can help you design dialogue and master the fundamentals of communication.

The guidelines in this section are concepts that form scaffolding for dialogue and the building blocks of conversation. Like equipment and materials used in various stages of building and restoration, they are meant to provide an environment conducive to the process of dialogue. They are based on sound principles and practice.

Why do leaders stop learning and repeat costly mistakes? Sometimes it's easier than exploring new ways of thinking. It takes hard work to abandon long-entrenched habits, shift, and reflect individually and collectively before taking action.

You operate from habit and inertia during most of your waking hours. You're not even consciously aware of what you're doing. If you want better results, you have to kick yourself out of your comfort zone into the learning zone. That's why it's important to review the concepts most relevant to dialogue, leadership, and transformative change.

Meaning, relationships, and transformative learning

The previous section reviewed dialogue as a stream of meaning flowing among, through, and between people. Making meaning together is the foundation of effective dialogue. It is also the basis for transformative learning, which is the process of using previous interpretations to construct a new or revised interpretation of present experience and future action. It's how people transform frames of reference that have become habits of mind, and that they therefore take for granted.

Your values and sense of self are anchored in your frames of reference. Therefore, your frames of reference tend to be emotionally charged. Not surprisingly, your inclination will be to strongly defend those frames of reference. Transformative conversations are perhaps the most effective way to achieve transformative learning and move organizations into a new future.

For transformative learning to occur, individuals must change their frames of reference by first reflecting critically on their assumptions and beliefs. They must also make a conscious plan for action. This is why sitting through a seminar or listening to a presentation does not lead to learning and change. Unless there is opportunity for critical reflection and conscious action, no change will occur.

Transformative learning is not just rational. It relies on the affective dimension of knowing, such as developing empathy toward others' viewpoints and trusting intuition. Once people validate and work through their emotions, they can begin the process of critical reflection.

A significant personal event that includes an emotional experience can trigger transformation. Emotional moments are common in transformative conversations. This explains why it's easier to learn within the context of dialogue. Integrating circumstances can also set transformation in motion. These are indefinite periods where people consciously or unconsciously search for the missing piece in their life. The transformation process occurs when they discover the piece. This is a subtle, emotional process that provides the opportunity to explore and clarify past experiences.

Neuroscience shows that mental training and practice can bring about changes in brain function. Emotions can help or hinder that process. Evidence also shows that deriving joy from activities is critical to learning, and to sustaining the learning. The brain's neuroplasticity makes lifelong learning possible. Nevertheless, the brain needs new challenges to keep it at its optimal capacity for learning.

Learning is also relational. A dialogue provides opportunities for people to contribute, question, explore, and experiment. The responsibility for learning is shared between all participants. In this way, learning relationships are mutually rewarding for the group. The elements of trust, friendship, and support can have an important impact on transformative learning. Dialogue, with its strong relational component, provides fertile soil for learning through relationships.

"Reflection" is the critical word for learning. Without it, change and transformation are not possible. It is through critical reflection that we challenge the validity of our thinking, assumptions, and prior learning. It is also through reflection that we open space for the new to be born.

Learning in the "Zone of Proximal Development"

Russian genius Lev Vygotsky developed another learning theory, the Zone of Proximal Development. Put simply, this theory refers to the range within which a child can learn in relationship with another person. It is bound on one side by the level of the child's independent functioning, and on the other by his or her functioning as a partner in an instructional social interaction.

Elaborating on Vygotsky's concept, Bruner added the term "scaffolding" to describe the supportive adult actions aimed to help the child's learning efforts. Though scaffolding might suggest a rigid structure, in this sense it is flexible. It implies a continuous revision of action in response to the child's activities that occur within a structured relationship.

For Vygotsky, development and activity are closely related. Although the activities a child can engage in are somewhat determined by the child's biological capacity, they are also greatly influenced by the cultural and historical traditions surrounding the child. At the same time, action is related to learning, and can influence development.

An interrelationship exists between learning, action, and development. Children must learn in order to be motivated, and learning leads to development, which never ends. Meaning making leads to ongoing development. Thus, transformation is the rule, not the exception, of life.

Although these concepts regard childhood development, they have implications for adults. When a leader develops an intentional scaffolding of conversations to expand options for making meaning, new learning and transformation can result. The way a leader encourages action while he supports his subordinates' efforts can result in talent retention and development. The way a facilitator designs the process of dialogue can spark learning, development, and transformation. Scaffolding can be seen as constraining, but it also offers the flexibility and safety needed for new developments and restoration to occur.

Dialogue versus discussion

Dialogue is the glue that holds relationships and organizations together. As Peter Block, a consultant, speaker, and the author of "Flawless Consulting," said, "What really matters in our lives is measured through conversations." Dialogue is an open-ended dynamic process that continues to flow even after individuals physically separate, as people tend to further reflect on what happened while they were together.

To better understand this concept, consider Beth's experience in this example. After Beth spent a morning engaged in dialogue about diversity, she continued to think about the dialogue and could hear the collective voices making new meaning. Here's how she described her experience:

> "Until that dialogue happened, I thought I was an open-minded individual with very few biases. The dialogue made me reflect. By listening to the different voices, I had to acknowledge – even though it pained me – that I have more biases than I was aware of previously. Although I'm not happy with that discovery, I feel I'm now more willing to acknowledge differences and explore my assumptions."

People tend to use the words "dialogue" and "discussion" interchangeably, but their meanings are quite different. Dialogue suggests a stream of meaning flowing among, through, and between people. This makes it possible for new understanding to emerge. In dialogue, groups make meaning together.

Discussion, on the other hand, is to shake apart what others say. In a discussion we break things down, fragment the whole, analyze the pieces, and compete to convince others of our insights. Everyone hastily offers viewpoints. People involved in discussion don't actually listen or attempt to understand. They only listen to prepare counterarguments. Here's the difference:

Dialogue	Discussion
-Starts with listening	-Starts with talking
-Is about speaking with…	-Is about talking to…
-Focuses on insights	-Focuses on differences
-Is collaborative	-Is adversarial
-Generates ideas	-Generates conflict
-Encourages reflection	-Encourages quick thinking
-Promotes emergence	-Promotes lock-in

Discussions don't bring understanding or foster learning, as you've likely observed in too many meetings. As one side throws a viewpoint across the table, the other retorts with a counter position. Back and forth it goes, like a Ping-Pong match. By contrast, dialogue encourages meaning to emerge. Dialogue leaves people feeling connected and energized, rather than frustrated and angry.

The design and building blocks of dialogue

Transformative conversations require both a solid design process and the fundamentals of dialogue. Several basic skills live at the core of dialogue, and it's important to learn and practice these skills for meaning making and transformation to occur.

Think of the skills in this section as reminders rather than rules. They're reminders to pay attention to thoughts, feelings, communication, assumptions, and judgments. They're triggers to note others' authenticity, conversational pauses, and meanings as they unfold. It takes attention to be open and collaborative. The mutual process of dialogue demands it.

Held lightly, the skills we explore will ease you into dialogue. Grip too tightly and they will trap you into a limiting system. Dialogue is a living process. It calls for you as the leader to let go of the known and discover new perspectives. When you have similar expectations for others, you will discover an exciting new world of possibilities.

The building blocks are grouped into three big categories: stop, start, and sustain. Depending on your personality and preferences, some skills will be easier to master than others. Find a systematic way to focus your practice on the skills that don't come naturally to you, and then practice until they develop into positive communication habits.

As you read about dialogue design and the building blocks of dialogue, think about your team. Use what you learn to strengthen your team. Let your attention be your blueprint as it guides you to new levels of meaning. These skills will soon become your path to effective communication.

5   *Designing Dialogue*

E FFECTIVE MEETINGS HAVE AGENDAS. They keep topics tidy and discussion on track. They also provide a format for developing action items. Agendas work well for teams managing routine issues. Complex challenges require something far more dynamic and robust than a simple agenda. They call for a dialogue design.

The process of dialogue design

A successful dialogue is the result of a well-crafted dialogue design. The time structure can be fluid, but the design has to be solid. Although each conversation will be different, you can follow these steps as you design your dialogue:

1. Identify participants

For an effective dialogue to occur, it's critical to include the right people. The ones who do the work and those impacted by the work can provide excellent insight. Ask yourself what voices need to be heard. Think big, and consider all stakeholders. Ask yourself the following questions.

- Who has a stake – either positive or negative – in this topic?
- Who is most affected by the issues we need to explore?
- Who has concerns?
- Who has nontraditional views on this topic?
- In relation to the issues, who are the opinion leaders?
- Who owns the knowledge?
- Who might champion ideas that emerge from the dialogue?

2. Secure and prepare the physical space

Physical space has a significant impact on conversation. Finding the *right* space is easier said than done. People are used to sitting theatre style in rows or around conference tables with the leader perched at one end. That kind of setup may fit spatially in a room, but it's not necessarily conducive to free interaction. It may inhibit dialogue.

Instead, use your creativity to bring a natural flow to the space. Arrange a circle of comfortable chairs on one side of the room and clusters of café tables elsewhere. The tables are perfect for breakout sessions. Include easel-size paper on each table so the groups can jot down ideas and drawings.

To give the circle some pizzazz, place a low round table in the center. Drape it with a special tablecloth. Place a colorful rug beneath it. Arrange attractive conversation pieces on top the table. They can serve as metaphors for the gathering. Things like a candle for understanding, a container with chocolates for nourishment, flowers or some other splash of color for creativity. The possibilities are only limited to your imagination. Participants can also bring objects to symbolize their intentions for the meeting.

3. Send an invitation

Make your invitation clear and compelling. You want attendees to truly join in the conversation, and it starts with the invitation. Explain why you're inviting them, tell them the time commitment, and let them know who will be there. As you compose the invitation, use these prompts to make it extra effective.

- Why are we having this conversation? Do we need to address a topic or a problem? Or, am I simply providing an experience?
- What is the major focus, expectation, and activity?
- Who needs to be present? Why? Can people send substitutes, if necessary?
- How long will it take? Will follow-up commitments be required?
- What are the logistical details? Are travel arrangements needed?
- What's the dress code?
- Will meals be provided?

A clear invitation will attract the right people. They'll arrive with solid expectations so they can respond to and influence the intention of the conversation.

4. Frame the conversation

It's important to frame the conversation so participants see the topic with fresh eyes. The frame you use to tell your story and ask questions will create reactions and cue specific responses. Develop your frame by crafting questions that get to the heart of issues, not symptoms.

Heed caution when designing questions. They can limit or widen the scope of possibilities for discovery. Design questions that can lead to solutions. Involve managers in a pre-meeting to brainstorm questions. Group questions into themes, refine them, and use them to fuel the conversation.

Be sure to frame issues with open and curious questions, with the goal of helping the conversation move forward. This will shift people away from debating opposing views and relying on their cherished beliefs. It will be easier to make meaning together as they move into a real meeting of minds and hearts.

5. Provide high interaction

Keep your goal in mind. You are designing a conversation. Not a presentation. Not a speech. You can begin to establish this in the way you craft the invitation. Then avoid the temptation to kick it off with a long speech. Leaders sometimes mistakenly assume they need to provide an expert monologue to confirm the meeting's importance. Instead, start with a highly interactive welcome exercise. It will set a great tone.

Keep this rule of thumb handy. Within the allotted timeframe, dedicate 65 percent of the time to conversation and 15 percent to reflection. That leaves 20 percent, which is ample time for harvesting results and designing an action plan.

6. Assign space for big and small group conversations

The big circle encourages coherence and reflection. It's perfect for introducing a subject and harvesting what's occurring. It's the small group that's most effective at addressing difficult issues and moving to action. Groups should be intimate enough to allow members to fully share and explain their ideas. People need to be able to probe. On the other hand, the group needs to be large enough to elicit creative content. Consider having groups of four, five, or six participants.

7. Keep conversation alive in small groups

For each topic, the table owns the conversation. Not the people. You might choose to allow several rounds of conversation for each issue. If so, let each round flow for 10-15 minutes. When time is up, have one person remain as the table's anchor. The other participants should randomly flow to other tables. At the conclusion, harvest the learning and create an action plan for implementation. Changing tables is a great way to help participants experience varying perspectives. It encourages open-mindedness.

It may be more convenient to keep the small groups together through-out the discussion on a particular issue. The key is to be aware of the conversational flow. When it is losing steam, stop. Wrap up while the conversation still has some life left it in. You'll have a better outcome than if you let energy levels plummet.

8. Get involved

If you're leading the meeting, don't be afraid to get involved. Contrary to conventional wisdom, your participation in small group discussions will not inhibit conversation. By participating as an equal at the table, you will encourage the concepts of mutuality and equality. Participating will also give you a voice in the conversation.

9. Encourage connection and meaning before content

Small groups connect people. They're more effective than ice breakers or round robins. When a group begins to work on a difficult issue, the members need to gain a sense of each other. What skills do these people bring? What's the experience level? What are their hopes? Connection first. Content second.

Participants will design better questions and offer stronger solutions if they first have the opportunity to connect. People value the chance to establish familiarity with their peers. They come to quickly understand each other's strengths and weaknesses. Sharing can influence in powerful ways. It can shift mindsets and lead to impressive creativity.

What other factors contribute to successful conversations?

A well-designed dialogue can result in fulfilled participants. You can expect them to feel that important issues were addressed and dealt with constructively. They may feel satisfied that their voices were heard. Most people appreciate the opportunity to share solutions and weigh in on action plans.

As you address organizational challenges, remember that the organizational response is not always best crafted in the senior leadership meeting. However intelligent and experienced the leaders, they lack diversity of thought. These diverse thoughts live in the organization – within departments, among teams, at every level and rank. As you become a conversation architect, you will benefit from the transformative conversations that emerge and the refreshing thoughts that follow.

With a solid process in place, it's time to key in on other important factors linked to successful conversations. You may not be able to achieve perfection within each category. However, you can expect richer dialogue when you insert more success factors.

Diversity

The most successful companies recognize and harness the power of diversity. When a workforce is diverse, its ideas, processes, dialogue, and products are diverse. Though diversity can bring moments of tension and disagreement, it leads to new ways of thinking.

Companies that value diversity have diverse customer bases, and therefore a competitive advantage in the global marketplace. According to Benjamin Akande, dean of the George Herbert Walker School of Business, "Organizations which are sufficiently bold and astute to recognize the strategic value and competitive advantage of diversity and inclusion will own the marketplace in the 21st century."

At its most basic level, diversity is difference among people and tolerance for people of different backgrounds. According to C.V. Harquail of Authentic Organizations, diversity can be broken into the following categories:

> *Identity – social and demographic diversity*: Includes social-physical features such as race, physical ability, gender, sexual orientation, generation, and ethnicity.

> *Cognitive – informational diversity*: Includes work experience, judgment, categorization, learning styles, perception, and intelligence.

> *Values – belief systems*: Includes value preferences, speculation about what's right, and attitudes toward the organization and the world.

> *Behavioral – personality styles*: Includes working methods and interactions with others.

Dialogue will undoubtedly benefit the organization as diversity proliferates in the workforce. Diverse viewpoints are required to tackle complex issues. Growing numbers of women, minorities, intergenerational workers, and persons with different lifestyles and ethnic backgrounds will bring fresh light to long-held processes and beliefs.

Consider the diversity that's already present in your organization. The diverse brilliance that already lives within your company could lead to a competitive advantage. Someone outside of the traditional corporate structure – a landscaper, security guard, intern – might provide just the insight you need to move forward.

Happiness

As you design dialogue, remember to keep the space positive and happy. It will lead to productive relationships, which will foster creativity. People need to enjoy the conversation. It's really that simple. You create a more joyful environment when you are happy and laugh. This kind of vibe creates feelings of solidarity and cohesion among coworkers. It reduces tension and provides a non-threatening environment.

Children laugh and smile about 400 times per day. Older adults, on average, break into giggles only 15 times daily. That's a sad statistic. Guess who has a better day? Infuse humor and its byproduct, laughter, into your conversational design. It will promote a positive focus, which is the hallmark of great leadership. As you develop your design, be mindful of laughter's many benefits:

Well-being: Laughing reduces blood pressure and stress while increasing muscle flexion. It also kicks endorphins into gear. They're the body's natural painkillers. Laughing brings relaxation and a sense of well-being. People in this state perceive others as more agreeable and friendly.

Clear thinking: Lighthearted people are more likely to be successful. Their positive feelings produce increased oxygen, endorphins, and blood flow. This helps them think clearly and creatively. If the conversation gets too heavy, inject a quick dose of humor to reset thinking and bring the conversation back on track.

Creativity: Laughing helps clear the brain's cobwebs so creativity can flow. Great leaders know this secret. Leverage the positive power of healthy humor in your teams. Then watch creativity blossom.

Soften difficult messages: George Bernard Shaw said, "If you're going to tell people the truth, you'd better make them laugh. Otherwise, they'll kill you." Do you have a colleague who takes 10 minutes out of a meeting to make a 30-second point? When he later gripes about the meeting's length, say, "The meeting could have ended on time if you would have made your contribution half as long." Point made. Direct attack avoided.

Solve tough problems: Unplanned humor can move a group toward a solution. Your attitude as a leader is contagious, and it's your role to set the tone. When you are optimistic and take challenges in stride, people around you will develop creative solutions to difficult problems. *The "in" dress for summer didn't fly off the racks as anticipated? Repackage it and market it as a Halloween costume!* It may not work as a practical idea, but it will certainly spark new ideas. Others will rise to your expectations when you appeal to their creativity.

Encourage shared responsibility

It can't be overstated: as a leader, your conversations become relationships. When you take responsibility for your thoughts, emotions, and messages you will speak with clarity, conviction, and compassion. The same is true for everyone in the dialogue circle. The way people feel post-conversation will determine their willingness to develop relationships further. People make countless excuses for conversations gone wrong. Have your direct reports complained that their colleagues were:

- Abrasive?
- Annoying?
- Entitled?
- Challenging?
- Nasty?
- Insulting?
- Oblivious?
- Out of control?
- In my face?
- Fill in the blank…

Obviously, you can't control how every individual in your organization acts. However, you can model mature, responsible, and accountable behavior. Others will follow your example. It starts with gaining awareness for the way you craft your thoughts. Rather than tell yourself, "In light of this merger, everyone is out of control," remind yourself that you can make a positive difference in the way the merger message is communicated to staff.

By taking control of your thoughts, words, and behaviors you will convey your willingness to contribute to the process. You may be surprised at your power to influence. Above all, don't let trivial matters sabotage a time for connection. Adopt a positive attitude and stick to it. Here are some techniques:

- Instead of saying negative things, ask questions that bring out the best in others.
- Publicly make positive comments.
- Resist the urge to say negative things to an annoying person. Just lighten up and ask the person to share a story.
- Rather than take a comment personally and give a nasty retort, offer a compliment.

By now you know that reflection is indispensable for learning and change. Yet, in the bustling world of business, many leaders see it as unnecessary. They fail to see how reflection impacts the bottom line. Reflection can help hold the mind's door open long enough for new concepts, connections, and solutions to emerge. Dialogue teaches people the importance of pausing mid-day to ponder recent events. It can provide a much-needed break for reading, asking questions, exercising, or relaxing. Even a short pause can bring meaningful perspective.

While leading dialogue, take ample time to reflect upon the group's work. They will form the habit too, leading to a culture of reflection. Ask yourself:

- Does my dialogue design include a reflective process?
- Do we take time as a group to identify missed and possible opportunities?
- Do I encourage people to reflect as they're taking action?
- Do I insert pauses into my meetings and dialogue?
- Do my current practices have soft spots? Where can I improve?
- Do I provide thoughtful feedback and encourage others to reflect?
- Do I pivot when reflection suggests it's time for change?
- Do I use self-evaluation and group-evaluation forms to enhance reflection?

Most people think they don't have time to reflect. Maybe you're one of them. Challenge yourself to find a quiet place in your mind, and then set aside the noise. Connect with your personal reflecting pool. You will begin to find and reach deeper truths while tapping into the energy and creativity that reflection can bring.

As you introduce reflection into your dialogue design, envision examples of it leading to bigger, better outcomes. During dialogue, give participants a moment to think before answering. Constantly remind yourself that meaningful conversations need breathing space. Insight happens in the space between words. It's that very insight that will lead to solutions and propel your business forward.

6 Stop: The First Building Block of Dialogue

IT TAKES A CONCERTED EFFORT to come to a full and complete stop. Have you ever approached a stop sign and rolled on through it? Maybe once? Or perhaps often? If you're an expert of the rolling stop, you're not alone. It can seem like an absurd waste of time to completely halt when there's no visible traffic. It's a symptom of our busy culture. We're in a rush. Too busy for contemplation, observation, and correct behavior.

It can be challenging to stop and learn from actions, reactions, and decisions. Yet, you will realize untold benefits when you do so. It's important to stop during different moments of a conversation, and you will learn here how to use your stop to pause, suspend, and listen.

Pause

What's a pause? It's when you take a moment to stop, to consider, to suspend reaction, and to reflect. In dialogue, a pause includes being silent, thinking, and reflecting. If you've ever played an instrument or appreciated music you understand the importance of pauses. They establish mood, transition, anticipation, and pace. Skillful composers use silence to build anticipation. Some of music's finest moments are spent in transition.

In 2007 a team of Stanford and McGill University scientists made an interesting finding. They watched the brain images of 18 volunteers listening to a series of movements within symphonies, each punctuated by frequent pauses. One- to two-second breaks between movements triggered a flurry of mental activity. As the music resumed, action shifted to different parts of the brain, and then subsided. "The pause itself becomes the event," said neuroscientist Vinod Menon of Stanford's School of Medicine, the senior author of a paper published in the journal *Neuron*. "A pause is not a time where nothing happens," he said.

The research team's findings have implications beyond concert halls. They shine a light into what neuroscientists call segmentation processes. This is the technique the brain uses to take a stream of sensory information and parcel it into comprehensible pieces. Likewise in dialogue, stillness deepens awareness, emergence, and integration.

Thinking and responding effectively takes time. However, processing time is essential for learning to occur. Technology can tempt you to believe that responding faster is better. Doing so can create a senseless cycle of chatter.

Imagine an international company that has teams of people from different cultures. A common practice is to interchange emails between team members on tasks and issues. The level of expertise is high. The cultural differences many. In this scenario it's common for people to misinterpret emails, be offended, and shoot an immediate scathing reply. Things can quickly escalate and become ugly.

Now, change the scenario. Imagine someone receiving an upsetting email and responding with a pause instead of a knee-jerk reaction. If the person lets it rest for a bit, re-reads it, and makes a phone call for clarification, the results could be more productive. This approach might result in a better understanding and working relationship, as well as higher team effectiveness.

When you take time to pause, clarify, and develop your thoughts, your contributions will be more valuable and effective. Here are some good reasons to pause:

> *Pauses invite learning.* It takes time to process, sort, compare, and analyze new data. As you pause you will gain insight into what you think and what leads you to think.

> *Pauses bring clarity.* Periods of silence allow for objectivity, discernment, and breakthroughs. As you quiet yourself, you will hear the soft murmurs of collective wisdom.

106

Pauses create a space. Listening can occur in this space. Pausing provides the opportunity to see beneath the surface and pay attention to "the space between." Creativity emerges from the in-between spaces.

Be silent

Silence is a state. It's a quiet resting period void of speech or noise. William Penn put it best when he said, "True silence is the rest of the mind; it is to the spirit what sleep is to the body, nourishment and refreshment."

It takes extreme discipline to observe, be silent, and avoid the temptation to interrupt. Some leaders react quickly and rapid-fire their thoughts, or simply speak to fill silence. You can manage this impulse if it's your personal challenge. While continuing to listen, just jot a note to release your thoughts. You will view silence as an ally once you master this skill.

Silence is an open space from which new sounds can emerge. It's a space that allows everyone time to breath, process, regain calmness, and formulate valuable questions. Silence becomes more natural and comfortable as dialogue deepens and individuals establish trust. There is a difference between speaking to fill the silence and speaking from the silence.

In dialogue, you intentionally keep silent when someone else speaks. You also pause before responding. Take a breath before you speak. Look deeply at what is being said or at what you are about to say. Notice what arises as you think about the words. Examine their meaning. Do you accurately understand the experience that is being conveyed? Are you accurately describing your experience? As you think about ways to use silence effectively, ask yourself these questions:

- How comfortable am I with silence? What personality traits or former experiences contribute to my ability or inability to be silent?
- In dialogue, do I remain silent when others speak?
- Could more silence add value to my interactions?
- How might my team use silence to increase effectiveness?

- If I began a meeting with 10 minutes of silence and invited others to write down their questions and thoughts, what dialogue might emerge?

As you employ silence as a tool for effective dialogue, notice the change that arises. You will begin to think more deeply about your words and what is actually being said. Examine the meaning. This process will lead to a richer understanding of the experience, and produce better results.

Think

Human beings create their reality through thoughts. Thinking leads to action or inaction. A pause is often needed for creative thinking to occur. During a pause, the mind explores its understanding of a concept and formulates understanding into a fresh expression. This all takes time, as information processing involves multiple cognitive tasks.

During ongoing dialogue, pauses give participants time to consolidate their thoughts and form new interpretations. Pauses also allow people to elaborate existing meanings and reflect on previous learning to determine if it's still relevant in the present.

Thinking also allows people to distinguish between the inferences they make about an experience, and the actual experiences. Harvard professor Chris Argyris developed the Ladder of Inference, a model later popularized in *The Fifth Discipline* by Peter Senge. This useful tool can help you reflect on your thinking.

The ladder of inference suggests our brains constantly absorb data, which we then process to create inferences about experiences. It occurs in an instant, and we're unaware of the process. We fail to notice the difference between a direct experience and our assessment of it. When we take action and arrive at conclusions, we don't realize that much more occurs in that instant. Here's how it works:

1. Our brains pick up pure data, like a photo, but there's no meaning attached.
2. Subconscious takes over. We begin to filter specific pieces of the picture.
3. We add meaning to the data based on our experiences and beliefs.

4. We draw conclusions from that meaning.
5. We adopt beliefs.
6. We take action based on those beliefs.

To test this, show three people the same picture. Ask them to tell you what it means. You will likely get three vastly different stories. The picture doesn't tell the story; however, each person's experiences and beliefs lead them to express a story. The stories people tell provide insight into their personalities and worldviews.

How does this work in business? Think about the Ladder of Inference, and consider these facts. You convene a meeting, but forget to notify your new hire. Her email wasn't in your list. When she doesn't show at the meeting, some may wonder why the new hire isn't present. Others may think she blew it off. Still others may think the new girl is already testing the waters. All of this occurs in a split second. People assume and judge based on what they believe is obvious and true. They can be wrong. Inferences can lead to serious mistakes.

On the other hand, someone could have asked about the new hire's whereabouts. This would have triggered you to remember that you forgot to notify her. You could have then called her, apologized, and invited her to the meeting. People have the tendency to take their original inferences as fact and not test conclusions, which can result in errors.

If you feel yourself moving too quickly up the Ladder of Inference, take a step back and reflect on your thinking. The Ladder of Inference presents an opportunity to see the difference between what we think and what has led us to that conclusion.

Reflect

To reflect is to give back an image, to think carefully, to ponder, to meditate, tocontemplate. Reflection allows you to think about, expand, reconsider, understand differently, develop, and transform your knowledge.

Superficial conversations and text messages seem to be the norm today. Leaders believe they should have answers ready for everything. Television, video games, and stress have programmed humanity's attention span. People bounce from subject to subject, and rarely pause to reflect or ask questions that could result in a deeper level of dialogue.

Dialogue deliberately slows the conversation so new understandings, appreciations, and meanings can emerge. When you reflect, you consider ideas and purposes, often with a willingness to understand and accept them. You look at things in their context and pause more frequently to let your mind assess the grounds of your beliefs.

You learn as you process and reflect on new information. You expand your knowledge as you make meaning of new data and connect it to your existing knowledge system. The more time you take to reflect, the more connections you will make at multiple levels.

Here is an example of how you can use personal reflection to better understand yourself, your work, and your role in an occurrence.

Recall a recent event where you had to use your leadership skills. Take time to reflect and answer the following questions:

1. What happened? What did I see? (Develop an objective account of the event, without inferences). What was my your role in the incident? What did or didn't I do?
2. What did I feel? What were my perceptions? What assumptions did I make? Did I check my Ladder of Inference?
3. How did I act? How did others react?
4. Analyze the incident. How did it affect me? How did it affect others? How did it change me?
5. What will I do the same or differently next time?
6. How can I apply what I learned to other situations?

Reflection is especially beneficial when it's necessary to have a difficult conversation. The greater the emotion attached to an issue, the greater the need for reflection. After taking action on a difficult issue, set time aside to reflect on the content, process, and premise of the conversation.

With the cooperation of others, you can correct distortions in your reasoning and attitude. You can also identify the strengths and weaknesses associated with your actions. Learning occurs in this way, and you can thoughtfully plan for better future performance.

Ideally and with practice, you should be able to reflect in action. This is the ability to see what happens as it happens. It's the ability to pause and reassess by asking, "What am I (or we) doing wrong?" Or, "What is going right?" Or, "How can we enhance performance at this moment?"

In this way, reflection becomes an integral part of thoughtful action. This is active reflection.

An exercise in pausing

The next time you're in a dialogue, pause intentionally for about 20 seconds to ask yourself the following questions. Doing this simple exercise will help you pay attention to something you might otherwise miss.

- Is there a new idea here? I want to pause to think about this.
- This needs some thought. What is the basis of my conclusion?
- Am I assuming? It's time to slow down and consider my ladder of inference.

A pause is not in reaction to anything. It's simply the result of your intention to pause. You decide to pause because you want to, not because something forces you to stop. Be aware of your thoughts. Make sure you know where they are coming from and how they are impacting your life and work. Then, take responsibility for your thoughts and actions.

Take time to pause, to value silence, and to listen to your internal dialogue and the external words of others. It's important to deliberately set aside time for personal and group reflection and renovation.

Suspend

Suspension is difficult because it requires you to relax your grip on certainty. Leaders typically like to feel they are "right." When you suspend, you do not work though out all of your thoughts in advance. You are willing to be influenced by the conversation. You acknowledge and observe thoughts and feelings without acting on them. You learn to reflect in action. You see what is happening as it happens.

Suspension requires you to live your dominant discourses – what you know or think you know – suspended, hanging out in front of you and everyone else. It requires that you not understand too soon, and that you let go of early assumptions and stereotyping thoughts. It demands that you open your mind to change and the unexpected.

What do you need to suspend? You need to suspend assumptions, biases, and judgments.

Suspending assumptions

Assumptions are difficult to see because you take them for granted or accept them as true even without proof or backup. Assumption is a supposition. It can make people presumptuous and arrogant. It's the snap evaluation you make when you say, "He's a good (or bad) person."

Because each individual has a unique life experience, each person carries a unique set of assumptions. But groups and cultures also have shared assumptions that glue people together. Different assumptions don't create problems; the need to be *right* about assumptions causes trouble. Effective communication demands that assumptions be tested and clarified. Only then can shared meaning evolve.

Individual or organizational assumptions can limit progress and cause costly conflicts. Assumptions are like bullets that can destroy and kill. Here is a sampler of assumptions that can confine dialogue and prevent its flow:

- "If my boss is being nice to me today, he must want something. I better be careful."
- "Investors don't care about our values."
- "I'm too old to learn that new system."
- "Beware, all people from (pick any city) are (pick any adjective)."
- "I can't afford to invest in new learning."
- "You must be trying to get my job."
- "This organization is going to fail if we keep talking about innovation."

You make assumptions every day. For example, when you drive you assume other drivers will obey traffic signals. Most drivers do, and so you proceed through intersections safely. Your assumption is right most of the time. However, it could be proven wrong and result in severe consequences. It's easy to see the assumption in this simple example. Assumptions are harder to see and understand in more abstract instances.

A good method for uncovering assumptions in any situation starts with thinking about the origins of assumptions. There are at least four possible origins of assumptions:

1. Cultural Through birth, family of origin, country, and the place where you live, you are immersed in influences – both subtle and not so subtle – that give privilege to one idea over another. This results in your cultural heritage. Consequently, you might prefer new over old, Western over Eastern, male over female. You could further prefer Mexican over Indian food, classical over rock music, and Christian over Muslim faith. The cultural divide between affluence and less privileged backgrounds is another huge influence.

This is how it works in my case. Because I have lived in five different countries and visit many others, I prefer to live and work with diverse and multicultural populations over homogeneous ones. Because I was born in Cuba, a Caribbean island, I prefer warm to cold places, an ocean with clear and warm waters, and natural places with green vegetation over deserts. Because I was raised in a communist country, I value freedom of expression and equality over hierarchical and repressive systems.

My life circumstances shape how I see the world, and how I interpret and understand ideas, people, and events around me. The same holds true for you. The cultures you and I inhabit all contribute to our way of thinking and form the basis for many of the assumptions we make about the world. I say cultures because each of us simultaneously inhabits several cultures at any one time: family, country, and workplace, to name a few. Culture is definitely a powerful originator of assumptions.

2. Biological Your genetic makeup is another source of influences, feelings, and preferences. Human beings associate being up and upright with good, while down and low with bad. Why? Mostly because of biology. When you are healthy, you are upright and erect. When you are ill, you are supine, lying flat, or lying low. You see "feeling on top of the world" as more desirable than "feeling down in the dumps." As a result, you might tend to prefer and follow leaders who are taller, and who you can "look up to," even though a shorter person might have the same or better qualifications. This is just a small example biologically determined assumptions.

Another way biology influences your assumptions is by the sensory pathways you prefer to use to receive and process information (think your five senses), and your cognitive preferences. It's important to be aware of those preferences so you are not blindsided.

3. Intellectual   Human beings have the unique ability to reason. Consequently, you might think you prefer fact over opinion, certainty over uncertainty, reason over emotions, and "truth" over "lies." The problem you face is that statistics can bend to tell half-truths. Neurobiology shows that "rational" decisions are impossible without the often unconscious input of emotions.

For example, If you make the faulty assumption that "pictures don't lie" without further investigation, you might later discover the picture was doctored in Photoshop. If you don't suspend and evaluate your assumptions, you might mistakenly make the wrong decision while thinking you are making a solid, rational one.

4. Idiosyncratic   You have a unique and distinctive history. Consequently, you may have past experiences that lead you to assume all politicians are controlling, all religions are dogmatic, or all people from the Midwest are unfriendly. These personal assumptions are predictable since they are usually based on traumatic or repetitive events in your personal stories. These same factors could lead you to make assumptions about sex, race, and age.

To further complicate things, some assumptions have supporting evidence and seem warranted. Many others have no supporting evidence whatsoever, and are therefore unwarranted. Because of the four underlying sources of assumptions, you might believe you have supporting evidence, when it is really an unwarranted assumption.

Assumptions can also become limiting by interfering or blocking your ability to think clearly about a particular issue. For example, an accountant might tell herself, "I'm good at math, but I don't like English, so I can't learn to write." Or, "The bosses are keeping me totally out of the loop in this merger, this must mean they are planning to fire me and I might as well resign and look for another job." Or, "I don't know what the others think, therefore, I better keep my mouth shut because I don't want to get burned."

You can lose many opportunities when you behave as if your assumptions are true. Don't limit yourself. Check your assumptions!

An exercise in assumptions

Think about an upcoming situation or meeting that may be potentially difficult. Take time to:

- Think up and write down as many assumptions as you can, including ones you are already forming about the upcoming situation.
- Take a moment to think about your assumptions. What are they based on, and what are their underlying sources? What past experiences color your assumptions? What personality traits or cognitive preferences make you prone to think that way?
- How often, and with whom, do you tend to make similar assumptions?
- How can you make sure you check your assumptions in your upcoming situation instead of acting "as if" they were true?

Suspending biases

Biases are a one-sided perspective or preference toward a particular ideology or result. They have a tendency to interfere with the ability to be impartial, unprejudiced, or objective. Biases include attitudes, judgments, or behaviors that are influenced by a prejudice. A bias can be unconscious or conscious.

Most people like to think they are unbiased. Yet, having a bias is part of your normal development. Everyone needs a more flexible perspective in areas where they tend to be biased. Your brain, as an information processor, can exhibit cognitive biases. Here are some examples of possible cognitive biases:

Confirmation bias is the tendency to interpret new information in such a way that it confirms one's prior beliefs. Confirmation bias can even lead to denial if you ignore information that conflicts with your cherished beliefs. People unconsciously search for supporting evidence for their decisions, ignoring any refuting proof. For example, once a leader makes a decision he or she seeks evidence that confirms the decision, while ignoring information that goes against it.

Bandwagon effect is the tendency to do or believe things because many others do too. This can be manifested in groupthink. Groups experiencing groupthink do not consider all alternatives and they desire unanimity at the expense of quality decisions. Examples of business groupthink disasters are Enron, Northern Rock, Lehman Brothers, and HBOS. There's a well-publicized story about the HBOS risk manager who was censored for raising concerns regarding the company's strategy.

Loss aversion is the tendency for people to strongly prefer avoiding losses over acquiring gains. For example, many investors have not learned to prefer stocks over bonds even after 70 years in which the average return of stocks was four times larger than that of bonds. According to this explanation, bonds are preferred because they eliminate the risk of (subjectively) costly losses.

Selective perception is the tendency for expectations to influence perception. It is the personal filtering of what we see and hear so as to suit our own needs. For example, sports fans honestly don't see many of the infractions committed by their favorite team during a game. Emotions can be a particularly strong trigger for selective perception. If you learn of a disagreement between someone you like and someone you dislike, you will tend to side with the person you like unless the evidence against your friend is strong.

Anchoring is the tendency to rely too heavily on only one trait or piece of information when making decisions. This bias usually occurs when you try to make a decision and see the situation as very similar to a past event. The similarity can lead you to believe that making the same kind of decision will produce a similar outcome.

Either/or thinking fosters competition and exclusivity. Both/and thinking creates collaboration and innovation. It also prevents groupthink and encourages creative problem solving. By suspending assumptions and biases, you will be less prone to prejudiced judgments.

Suspending judgments

One of the worst problems with assumptions and biases is that they tend to lead to judgments. While judgment is sometimes useful, it tends to shut down dialogue, curiosity, the ability to see the whole picture, listening, and learning. Seeing beyond judgments is essential for reaching understanding.

Whether you agree or disagree with another person, your judgments will limit your ability to listen and learn new things. Strive to be aware of your judgments. In so doing, you can gain clarity and recognize your reaction. Then you can gain objectivity and bring your thought into the conversation as an interpretation.

Suspending judgments is about developing the ability to observe and recognize assumptions and biases in yourself and others from a neutral position, without forming precipitated judgments.

It is important to understand and recognize the difference between useful and harmful judgments. It is equally critical to recognize the difference between those that expand options and understanding, and those that limit them. Sometimes you may use a limiting leadership style or accept mediocre work from others due to your limiting judgment about others' capacity. On the other hand, if you suspend your judgment and try something different, things could change for the better.

By suspending and inquiring into assumptions, biases, and judgments, you open the space to listen for the emergence of shared meanings. It is important to engage in conversations about the assumptions underlying the structures and flow of information in the organization, and the ones that drive strategies, planning, and decision-making. This can be beneficial in clarifying issues and taking the organization to a higher level of performance.

Listen

Listening occurs with the eyes, ears, and heart. It facilitates understanding and appreciation. As you listen, you make a thoughtful effort to pay close attention. Because listening is at the core of interactive dialogue, it's helpful to learn to listen to your own listening. Become aware of *how* you listen. Listening is interactive, not passive. It prompts the speaker to come alive and sustain enthusiasm.

The quality of your listeningconveys a sense of appreciation, acceptance, and understanding. When you listen, the other person becomes responsive, comes alive, and sustains enthusiasm. You must be fully present to be a good listener. Let go of agendas. Release inner noise. Calm your emotions to listen with intensity.

Once you achieve this state, it will be easier to recognize how you color what others say. You will become keenly aware of meanings that surge from conversation. You will begin to listen for meaning that might impact not just you, but everyone involved.

Listen to understand

As a rule of thumb, strive to understand first and be understood second. We gain a shot of confidence when we receive confirmation that we understand something correctly. Listening is the first step for gaining understanding.

In Native American Society, the Plains Indians used talking circles to facilitate understanding. A concerned person would initiate a talking circle when he wanted the community to understand and address an issue. That concerned individual might enlist another person to convene the group and serve as moderator. This allowed the concerned person to listen carefully and understand.

Council members shared thoughts based on their individual perspectives. They used a talking stick, usually a feather or carved cane, to take turns. They believed that the person with the stick was connected to the spirit world through thought and energy. Shared meaning emerged and they expressed viewpoints. They built consensus subtly, as though a pile of words were arranging themselves in a meaningful way. All the while, the concerned person would listen intently. Not responding. Just listening.

Apply this concept to business. Take time and have the discipline to quiet your internal noise long enough to totally focus on what is being said. Put aside the resistances and reactions you might feel for the subject matter.

When someone has the chance to listen to multiple viewpoints, he can determine his follow-up actions accordingly. Other participants can likewise benefit as they file away meaning to use in future circumstances. When everyone listens to understand, they will not only hear the speaker's words, but also the meaning that evolves from the group.

An exercise in listening

Assess your listening by answering the following questions:

- What makes it difficult for you to fully tune in to dialogue?

- What makes you willing and able to fully listen? (It may help to recall a time when you were engaged in listening. What helped you listen in that circumstance?)
- What behaviors do you display when you are fully listening?
- Recall a time when you stopped listening. What closed you off to the conversation? How could you have listened differently?

To benefit the most from listening, try to listen for three aspects simultaneously:

Listen to what the speaker is saying. To understand meaning, identify important points and ask relevant questions until you and the speaker are satisfied you understand.

Listen to your listening. Tune into your internal conversation and your feelings about the external conversation. Your inner voice is filled with judgment. It develops ways to refute what you're hearing. This is why it's important to master suspension, so you can put your biases aside. Listen to your own voice – beyond your words to the message – when it's your turn to speak. If you are genuinely interested, people will communicate with you. Are you able to listen without resistance? What does it feel like?

Everyone has a different technique for staying in the moment. Some people contemplate quietly. Others speak a few words. Some people giggle nervously. Some shout. To help people remain in their moment, ask yourself why their train of thought differs from yours. Avoid the temptation to think they're disagreeing with you. Instead, ask yourself, "Why is that person thinking differently than me?" It will alleviate you from feeling defensive.

Listen together as themes emerge. As a leader, it's important to remember that what each individual feels, sees, hears, and perceives is only a corner of the reality. Recognize that diverse personalities and experiences contribute to a spectrum of thoughts. The multiple voices create a beautiful and rich symphony that brings a totally new meaning to the experience.

Problems can escalate when departments listen from their perspective. They assume they can fix the problem alone, or blame others and don't feel the need to contribute. In reality, departments might be contributing to other departments' problems in a repetitive negative cycle. People must listen together to see reality and improve the system.

Use these questions to help develop your skills in listening to collective meaning.

- Is there a common reality emerging from the different viewpoints?
- What are the different lenses creating diverse perspectives?
- What shared meaning is being revealed? What common story is emerging?
- What dilemmas are present? How can people face them so we can open doors?
- What would the song be if I could create one "track" with the perfect "mix" from all the different voices?

Common understanding and meaning will develop when you can listen together, taking into account how things look from others' perspectives.

Listen to connect

Hearing is the first sense humans develop and the last to go. A fetus' ears are fully functional at 20 weeks. The fetus can hear sounds inside the womb, as well as exterior music and voices. Studies show that a year after birth, children recognize and gravitate toward music they were exposed to in the womb.

What's more, linguists can detect differences in the cries of French versus German newborns. This is based on the notion that babies first learn via imitation in the womb. This underscores the important impact of native language. It also helps explain why babies recognize their parents' voices at birth. It is the first connection.

In business, people often admit to being angry or depressed because "no one listens." The greatest gift you can give as a leader is the gift of listening. Listening can be broken into three categories. Note the category that validates people and contributes to transformative conversations.

> *Listening, not hearing*: Your thoughts are elsewhere. This kind of listening can occur when someone interrupts you. Strengthen your relationship by saying, "Can we please talk when I can give you my undivided attention?" People respond well to honesty.

> *Listening, but connecting with your own agenda*: This occurs when you listen to confirm your ideas or find the weak spot in others' reasoning, so you can advance your ideas. In this sense, it's impossible to recognize new concepts.

> *Listening deeply*: This happens when you hear both the spoken word and the unspoken details. It happens when you listen with your ears, eyes, and heart. This listening strengthens connections.

Listen to appreciate

When you suspend, pause, and listen deeply, you gain a new appreciation for others in the dialogue. As you listen to appreciate, you will welcome people *and* their points of view. Human beings, regardless of background, experience joy and pain similarly. In this spirit, tune into your humanity and feel your biases, assumptions, and antagonisms dissolve. Sometimes the best way to solve a problem is to dissolve it.

I once worked with two partners who were ready to dissolve their business. The core issue: neither was listening to appreciate the other. They couldn't see beyond their differences. The one partner, who recognized he had been in several previous failed partnerships, decided it was time to take a different course. He would make an effort to save this partnership.

That set a new tone, and after working through issues together for several months, the partners regained their strength as a team. They adopted a new appreciation for their individual styles. They learned to listen with appreciation. The one partner said, "I'm amazed that once I got over myself it wasn't so difficult to really listen to my partner. I never dreamed that changing my listening style would make me feel so much happier."

Challenge yourself to listen as long as necessary to sincerely appreciate what others bring to the conversation. You will feel happier. The other person will feel valued.

7 Start: The Second Building Block of Dialogue

A S IMPORTANT AS IT IS to stop in dialogue, at some point it's necessary
to start taking a more active role. In fact, although the building
blocks are presented individually in this book, dialogue is not linear. It's
circular. Stops and starts occur continuously. It's your role as a leader to
inspire others to generate ideas and move them into action.

In football, players and coaches take time outs to review and strate-
gize. However, thoughtful reflection does not win games. The players
have to begin playing and play well. In that same sense, at some point
your team has to begin performing and perform well. They must overcome their fears and take the field.

On June 6, 1944, Brigadier General Norman Cota was the assistant
divisional commander of the United States 29th Infantry Division at Omaha Beach, Normandy. The landing at Omaha has gone down in history
as one of the most difficult and bloody. When troops were paralyzed by
fear and dying in droves at the beach, facing what seemed impossible to
overcome, he shouted, "There are only two kinds of people on this beach:
those who are dead and those who are going to die. Now, let's get the
hell out of here!" Under his command, the fearful soldiers moved inland.
The beachhead was secure by nightfall.

Any kind of movement, action, or start – even if feared – leads to
results. The men at Omaha won the day because they began walking while
they were terrified. Action eventually dislodged fear. To model Brigadier
General Norman Cota's words, "In the present business climate, there are
only two kinds of organizations: those who have failed, and those that
are going to fail unless they begin having transformative conversations to
move them forward!"

As a leader you need to be able to inspire people not only to generate ideas, but to bring them into action. To start, you must inquire, share, and cultivate. It's important to dissect each of these areas.

Inquire

When you inquire, you seek to know and understand. An attitude of curiosity stimulates new levels of understanding and learning. It opens up possibility and broadens perspectives. Breakthrough and innovation emerge because inquiry unveils new possibilities and can deepen your ability to think systemically. You have to ask the right questions for real learning and discovery to happen. Questions help you discover, learn, and be flexible.

In dialogue, you balance inquiry with intention and advocacy. Leaders who value transformative conversations use them to explore issues, share perspectives, formulate strategies, and make action plans. Then they execute, evaluate, and reflect. This constant process becomes integral to their leadership. It makes them mindful of the conversations they encourage and the questions they ask.

Ask questions

Have you ever noticed that you can lead better by asking questions than by providing answers? Several types of questions facilitate dialogue:

> *Information gathering questions.* When you inquire about an issue, collect facts through your senses and resist the urge to interrupt. Ask questions like, "You say Andrea was rude. Describe her rudeness. What was her tone? How did her face look?"

> *Open questions.* These encourage creativity and generate energy. You might say, "Given our challenges, how can we restructure our division to optimize our resources?" Questions like this will open the space for creative thinking and meaning making.

Possibility questions. These help people discover new territory. Sometimes leaders think they communicate clearly, but employees don't hear the message. Or employees only hear what can't be done.

Questions that take you to new places can help you communicate the possibilities of virtually any message.

1. *Who?* Who is responsible? Who has authority to make changes?
2. *What?* What is happening? Provide basic information to explain the big picture.

3. *When?* When will this take place? When will people need to know and be ready?
4. *Where?* Where are new resources available? Where is the idea going?
5. *Why?* Why does something need to be done or changed? Explain the rationale.
6. *How?* How will this impact the company and every employee? How will it be done?

A good leadership quality is the ability to reframe questions so they're focused on desired outcomes and possibilities rather than problems. Here are some examples.

Instead of saying: What is the biggest problem here?

Ask: What possibilities exist that we have not yet considered?

Instead of saying: Why do we have such a big problem with communication?

Ask: What small changes in our communication style could make the bigger impact?

Instead of saying: Why do you always blow it up with our clients?

Ask: How can we find solutions that lead to a positive outcome for you and our client?

125

Appreciative inquiry is another proven way to inquire in a way that brings out possibilities. David Cooperrider developed a school of thought on change. He called it appreciative inquiry, which has to do with the transformational power of appreciation. He says, "As people throughout a system connect in serious study into qualities, examples, and analysis of the positive core – each appreciating and everyone being appreciated – hope grows and community expands."

Appreciative Inquiry by its nature is a cooperative process that collects, builds on, and works with strengths and possibilities. It probes into stories of past success. It uses productive questions to help identify strengths and weaknesses. Then it uses questions that spur creative thinking. This helps people envision possibilities, which increases energy levels. It shifts the focus from roadblocks to pathways leading to success. Use these kinds of questions to help expand creative thinking:

> *What if*? This inspires vision and forward motion. "What if we could accomplish our goals in the manner we desire without having to worry about budget?" What would we do?

> *What else*? This encourages people to explore alternatives, rather than simply accept the first answer offered. "What else can we do?"

> *Why Not*? This removes constraints and frees the mind. "Why not try it for a week?" "Why not ask him directly?"

An exercise in inquiry

Set aside 30 minutes to immerse yourself in this process. Remove distractions. Working as quickly as you can, draft a list of at least 25 hypothetical questions for yourself that could change the way you work. Your goal is to ask the questions in the manner just described: *What if, what else, why not*? Write without stopping or judging. After 30 minutes, stop, read, and ask yourself the following:

- What are the most common types of questions I asked?
- How many questions are possibility questions?

- What else could I ask?
- If I did this for every area of my life, how would I change?
- What if I used this exercise with others at work?
- Can I write another 25 questions?

Nurturing a dynamic relationship between questions and curiosity frees people to invent, contribute, and adjust to a turbulent and changing world. Questions can help you see things with fresh eyes. Once you begin to ask questions differently, ordinary conversations will become transformative and lead to successful change.

Discover

Discovering meaning together creates trust and expands potential. Finding connections among distinct and different perspectives can give rise to innovative combinations. Yet, for discovery to happen you must be curious and open space to ponder questions, reflect, and consider. When you are in discovery mode, an answer does not signal the end of anything. It is the beginning of something else. There is much discussion about the need for discovery and innovation in today's marketplace. There is not enough dialogue around what it takes to fuel innovation.

Perhaps that's because innovation is not a thing, it's a mindset. It's a new way of thinking about business strategies. This thinking needs to be systemic in nature since it drives every aspect of a successful organization. It should penetrate every element of business. Your mindset is a result of your choices. If you're willing to change your mental models, you have the power to change your beliefs. This can enhance your capacity to innovate.

Dialogue is an ideal way to discover new meanings and explore mindsets. Highly creative companies provide staff with ample time to talk informally. Some of the greatest advancements have come from casual conversation. As you evaluate your own mindset, consider these strategies used by some of the most innovative leaders.

Disrupt comfort

Exit the safe, secure corner and take a risk. Veer from current strategies to discover capabilities that you never knew existed.

Dismantle certainty

Suspend your reality and train yourself to forget, and then relearn quickly. You can entertain multiple possibilities, inquire into the unknown, and create the unexpected. The innovation may surprise you.

Focus on new insight

Brainstorm. Collect ideas. Observe the unexpected. Entertain outrageous ideas. Tap diverse sources. Adopt a desire to understand how things function outside of your current perspective. Insight and innovation will follow.

Don't be afraid of failure

Fear of failure kills innovation. To lead a culture of successful and sustainable innovation, make failure your friend. Intelligent failure takes risks and creates the confidence required to abolish the fears that derail innovation. They are learning experiences.

Collaborate and communicate

Innovation is much more than developing bold new ideas. It also has to do with people championing new projects, making decisions, and negotiating meaning together. This requires effective communication and collaboration. It's why transformative conversations are crucial on the path to innovation.

Foster creativity

A creative mindset requires both lateral and out-of-the-box thinking. Give yourself and others permission to daydream and ask ridiculous questions. Become a child for the day. You might like what you see.

Encourage diversity

Diversity encompasses the whole human experience: age, race, gender, culture, education, personality skills, cognitive preferences, and life experiences, to name a few. Diverse people ask diverse questions that drive innovation.

As you reflect on these strategies for leading innovation, realize that the secret is not a well-guarded formula of mental faculties. It's a style for leading others in a dialogue where it's safe to explore, abandon, and twist previously held attitudes and beliefs.

Learn

Learning begins with values. It is strengthened and stretched as you ask questions, reflect, and engage in dialogue. The result is new knowledge and behaviors. The plasticity of the brain makes humans capable of life-long learning. We learn best when we engage our whole brain. This process facilitates transformational learning.

An Australian education and learning consultant, Dr. Julia Atkin sees learning as an integration of experiences, feelings, reflections, and actions. This is how she visualizes learning:

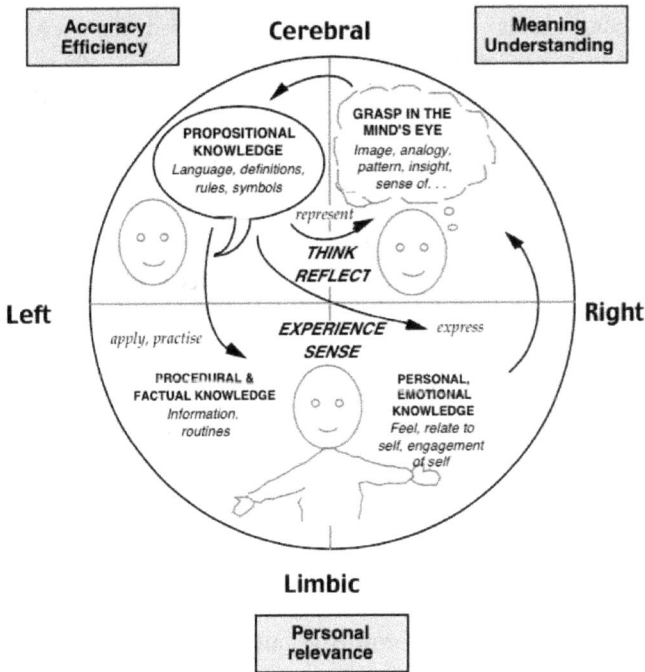

| Accuracy Efficiency | **Cerebral** | Meaning Understanding |

GRASP IN THE MIND'S EYE
Image, analogy, pattern, insight, sense of...

PROPOSITIONAL KNOWLEDGE
Language, definitions, rules, symbols

represent

THINK REFLECT

Left

Right

apply, practise

EXPERIENCE SENSE — *express*

PROCEDURAL & FACTUAL KNOWLEDGE
Information, routines

PERSONAL, EMOTIONAL KNOWLEDGE
Feel, relate to self, engagement of self

Limbic

| Personal relevance |

Dr. Atkin talks about integral learning and uses a whole brain model of learning. Consider the way children learn from birth. They imitate, explore, and express curiosity. This prompts endless questions. Their innate curiosity helps them learn. It's disappointing that many adults adopt the belief that curiosity is kid stuff. Is it because people in authority squash their questions? Is it because curious adults are perceived as childlike?

As a leader, it's paramount to encourage curiosity. It's the very thing that will lead to curious questions, and ultimately learning. When employees learn, they gain satisfaction, enjoyment, and a sense of healthy personal agency. These factors lead to increased productivity. The wisdom and capabilities of the learning organization are not measured in what it knows, but in how it learns.

Share

Sharing your thoughts, feelings, and dreams in your own voice may be the most challenging skill to develop. It requires courage to make your internal world visible. It's worth it. Sharing connects people, and increased connectedness leads to positive energy and increased effectiveness.

Sharing is one of the greatest gifts you can give others. Award-winning photographer and filmmaker Andrew Zuckerman shared this belief. He produced a brilliant book and film, *Wisdom: The Greatest Gift One Generation Can Give to Another*. It details the wisdom hunt he designed to learn from 50 great thinkers over age 65 – writers, artists, philosophers, politicians, designers, activists, musicians, religious, and business leaders. He asked seven questions and recorded his subjects' candid responses. The result was an intelligent, inspirational, and invaluable lesson on wisdom.

The greatest service you can offer other leaders and your organization is wisdom. This shows itself when you share your insights and dreams. You can accomplish this by sharing your:

- Stories of success and failure.
- Best-learned lessons.
- Deepest values and philosophy.
- Institutional history, knowledge, and insight.
- Hopes and fears for the future

Rather than hoard your knowledge and experience, share it openly. Choose to become vulnerable and share your inner self. Do it in your own voice. This personal advocacy can be challenging. It requires a special kind of courage to share what you think and feel instead of what you believe you should say. In one of its earlier usages, the word "courage" meant to speak one's mind by telling one's whole heart.

Being vulnerable can be scary. Exposing your heart can be terrifying. It exposes you to the possibility of attack. However, there will be rewards. As you reveal your authentic self and share what's in your heart, your confidence will increase and you will personally believe in your own wisdom. So will others.

Here's a great example of the positive that came from a courageous leader willing to share from his heart. This experience took place at a meeting I facilitated for the leadership group of a manufacturing facility. They were in dire need of a transformational change. People recognized that change was overdue, but they were cautious about how to proceed. Then the vice president who convened the meeting spoke up:

> I feel I'm the greatest obstacle for moving toward change and for you to show the willingness to step up and take ownership. In the past I may have been too quick to dismiss or criticize your ideas. You try to guess what I want, rather than suggest anything that might make me uncomfortable. Don't try to please me. Share what you think will be helpful. Don't worry about my reaction. I will try to be more open-minded.

His remarks opened up a dialogue that allowed others to fearlessly explore innovative ways to solve challenges. The other leaders began to contribute freely. They posed ideas about taking risks, exploring new models, and being responsive to market needs. The vice president's remarks sparked new energy and opened the flow of creativity. Instead of being perceived as weak, he gained instant respect.

Share your thoughts

Human beings have the ability to share thoughts in real time. There is value to this, especially during brainstorming sessions or emergency situations. There is equal value in having the skillset to plan your remarks. You know this if you ever regretted your words, the way you framed your words, or the stance you took due to peer pressure. You can avoid those moments of regret if you pay attention to your thoughts before you speak. Here's how:

- Keep your emotions in check. Don't let them speak for you.
- Listen to your internal dialogue and the surroundings.
- Resist the urge to focus on your response. Just be aware, absorb, and notice.
- Decide what to share. Maybe you'll dovetail off another person's comments and naturally continue the conversation.
- Be confident in your ability to sense when it's the wrong time to share.
- Craft your thoughts so others can receive them. Keep it concise and respectful.

It's important to find your own authentic voice. This process can take time, especially if you have silenced your voice as a result of prior negative feedback. You express your voice both verbally and non-verbally. It's critical to establish a voice with a soul, one that won't be silenced when it needs to be heard.

You reveal your thoughts and heart with your voice. As you speak, you create. You can conjure an image, paint an alternative scenario, or take people on an adventure. You can bring them into a story and make them part of the creative process.

An exercise in listening thoughts

As you develop your voice, pay attention to your thoughts and how you work with them throughout the day. Ask yourself these questions at the end of the day.

- Do I tend to withhold my thoughts?
- Who gives voice to my thoughts? Me? An outside influence?
- What do I risk by speaking out?
- What do I risk by holding back?
- How do I decide what thoughts to express?

Sharing your feelings

It's common for leaders to avoid thinking about feelings. They might perceive feelings as unimportant or as roadblocks to rational action. Feelings exist, whether ignored or not. The more you ignore their existence, the more they will interfere with your ability to lead, and the more likely you will be to send mixed messages. Communication is challenging enough without the insertion of mixed messages. They create a confusing disconnect. Here are three examples that illustrate their complicated nature:

- An employee agrees that a project is high priority, but a week later no progress has been made.
- A team member tells you he loves the project, but his expression and body language convey anger.
- You tell your manager you have time to listen, but continue to look at your computer.

It's crucial for your words to match your actions, just as it is for your message to match your head and heart. Speak with conviction, and then follow up accordingly. Engage your feelings so they don't sneak out and create confusion.

For example, don't rant and rave when you are angry. Don't belittle people when you feel frustrated with their behavior. Don't clam up and seethe inside when you feel disrespected. Don't cool your enthusiasm when you are passionate about a project. Don't look unconcerned when someone is hurting. Don't appear indifferent when you are bursting with joy. Challenge yourself to listen to your feelings and share them in a constructive way.

Consider the example of a leader who becomes angry when his team shows little concern for an important project's timeline. Rather than lash out in fury, he calms himself and listens beyond his feelings to discover:

- He is afraid of losing his job if he doesn't meet the timeline.
- He feels inadequate because he's unable to communicate the project's urgency.
- He believes his team thinks he's insensitive because he fails to explore roadblocks.

As a result of his reflection, this leader has an opportunity to change tactics. He can convey the project's urgency, brainstorm ways to put competing projects on hold, and inquire about progress.

Share your dreams

When you share your dreams, whether for a single project or a lofty goal, you establish a framework for innovation. Dreaming is a form of planning. Rather than consider your dreams frivolous, view them as an opportunity for discovery and a way to unlock creativity. As the famous women's liberation activist Gloria Steinem said, "Without leaps of imagination, or dreaming, we lose the excitement of possibilities."

Cultivate

Cultivate habits of mind that bring openness, curiosity, and flexibility. Open your mind to new ideas, methods, and opinions. Show the same curiosity you exhibited as a child. Flexibility will smooth the path for dialogue and understanding.

Cultivate openness

If you want to keep the lines of communication open, you must be flexible and humble enough to keep an open mind. Remember, you are not always right! Dialogue requires you to stand your ground while being profoundly open to new ideas and thoughts. Just as you express your opinions, feelings, values, and ideas openly and clearly, be willing to listen openly to others.

Why should you be open to those who think differently than you? Because when you listen with an open mind, you may learn more about your own beliefs, understand others better, and discover differences and similarities. You may also find that your concerns are similar to those with whom you disagree. Perhaps you will even learn to respect others more, discover new ways to be productive, reduce hostilities, and be able to work together despite your differences.

Dialogue requires a willingness to open your mind to see things from the other person's perspective. You can promote that type of openness in your emails, in the way you conduct your meetings, in the time you spend listening, in the physical spaces you create to encourage conversations, and in the inspirational messages you deliver at meetings.

It takes discipline to disregard your ego aside and remain open to hear and seek input. When you encourage openness in dialogue, you will help harvest your team members' diverse thoughts into something useful.

Cultivate curiosity

How can you cultivate curiosity, and why is it important? When you cultivate an attitude of curiosity and excitement, you facilitate open dialogue. The brain is wired for change and growth. Think again about childhood. Children are curious and ask many questions. They're surprised by discovery. They share wonder. They explore. In this same sense, dialogue is a mind exploration. When you're curious, you can experience unexpected pleasure as you wander through others' thoughts.

Contrary to the adage "curiosity killed the cat," research suggests that curiosity thrilled the cat! The brain likes surprises. Research shows that the brain's pleasure centers are more turned on when unpredictable pleasant things occur. Curiosity is rewarding because exploring new approaches is exciting. Plus, it can be invigorating to start a project when the end result is unknown.

The "eureka!" moments that come with innovation are rewarding because they arrive in the form of an unexpected surprise. When you keep a curious mind, it's nearly impossible to predict the end result of a conversation.

The area in the brain responsible for the pleasure derived from surprise is the nucleolus accumbens. It is linked to other parts of the brain that modulate cycles of reward for behavior. The nucleus accumbens is part of a set of neural pathways that facilitate learning new behaviors by pleasurable reinforcement. This explains why random reinforcements work well as motivators, and why predictable reinforcements are less effective.

That said, people do like predictable paychecks. However, people don't experience extra pleasure from receiving predictable pay. An unexpected bonus, even if modest, changes that. Keep your team motivated, creative, engaged, and learning by providing unexpected positive experiences. Here are a few ideas:

- Give an unexpected thank-you note.
- Leave a cup of coffee for a diligent assistant.
- Offer public or private recognition.
- Turn a boring meeting into a short fun gathering.
- Assign a creative project in the middle of a routine assignment.

Curiosity brings new growth

Everyone needs something new at some point. New clothes due to a change in weight. New friendships as a result of a move. A new job because the old one became stale. A new start because it's time for a redesign. New can be slow and gradual, like the arrival of a late spring. New can be dramatic, like a fierce storm bringing destruction. The aftermath requires complete reconstruction and healing.

New growth can be tiresome and exhaustive, like the toil the Pilgrims endured for the reward of living in a new land. At other times the new appears quickly and unexpectedly, like a sudden promotion or new friend who arrives dancing into your life at the perfect time. No matter how it comes, be willing and ready to embrace the new.

Prepare yourself by looking for possibilities. See beyond the senseless busywork and drudgery of the urgent and familiar to curious new ways of thinking and leading. As you take time to be curious and daydream, follow up by outlining a clear design and objectives. Be specific and realistic. Here are some tips:

- List the three most important areas where you want to grow.
- Write down why they are important to you.
- Choose one that you want to start right now. The best way to take action isto start as soon as you make the decision.
- Devise a reasonable plan to incorporate the new growth into your life.
- Examine how you might sabotage your plan. Formulate ways to prevent that.
- Be specific and realistic.

Start small and grow into the new. This will empower you to learn and grow. Beautiful flower gardens require dreams, design, attention, and careful work. Effective communication also needs cultivation. To be a successful leader, you need the drive and foresight to see blooming flowers in what may look like shy tiny plants. Though it's easier to act out of habit and ignore new ways of thinking, it's critical to be ready for the new. Here's how:

1. Keep your eyes and mind open to new possibilities.
2. Adopt a childlike curiosity.
3. Listen to your team, to experts, and to colleagues in various fields.
4. Make time to think, notice, question, learn, and cultivate.

Cultivate new directions of growth. By embracing this new mindset, you will be better prepared to keep pace with the relentless changes of global marketplace.

Cultivate flexibility

It can be hard to keep perspective. People grumble about problems while ignoring the good around them. Take for example my client. Let's call him Stan. He's a manager with a tendency to focus on the negative. He's working to change his perspective, see the positive, and speak his mind. He recently complained that his boss tried to embarrass him in front of the team.

> We've been discussing changes to company policies. I disagreed with one of the changes and spoke privately to my boss. He listened, but didn't change his stance. When he later presented his decision to the group, he explained the policy was going forward even though some people disagreed with it. He looked right at me and said, "Right Stan?" Why did he have to humiliate me like that?

I encouraged Stan to look at the incident from a different perspective. He admitted he could not see it any other way. When I told Stan that perhaps his boss was giving him permission to publicly disagree and explain his thinking, Stan was surprised. "Wow. That changes everything," he said. "If I look at it that way I feel empowered, not embarrassed."

Be flexible enough to shift your perspective. It can be refreshing and even reduce your stress. It can also help you relate to the person challenging you. Instead of a roadblock, see the opportunity to take a new path.

Think of yourself as a photographer. As you frame your picture, move around with your camera until it provides just the right perspective. Then shift slightly. Your new angle may totally change the scene. If you shift from being defensive to listening for the good in others' opinions, your work and life will be more enjoyable. As Henry David Thoreau said, "The question is not what you look at, but what you see."

8 Sustain: The Third Building Block of Dialogue

IT IS NOT ENOUGH to communicate effectively. Dialogue needs to be sustainable. This requires a strong, safe space where people feel competent and free to share. They must also feel a mutual trust and respect. What does a safe place for communication feel like? A safe place is a one where:

> *People can be vulnerable.* People can allow themselves to be vulnerable if they know others will embrace that vulnerability, not exploit it. Individuals can help each other overcome weaknesses.

> *People can talk without interruption.* Individuals value a space where they can complete their thoughts without interruption.

> *People listen with kindness.* Everyone makes mistakes when speaking. People who listen with kindness find ways to help others clarify their messages.

> *People show respect.* Participants can disagree with messages without attacking the messenger. A respectful place is void of personal attacks, screaming, cursing, and strong emotional outbursts.

Your leadership can help create a safe space where open communication is possible. You have to start by being willing to show your own vulnerability. By exemplifying and promoting the attributes that help create a safe space, you will help people feel free to share openly.

As a leader, you can certainly think of reasons why people stop speaking their truths. They may be fearful that no one will listen, or that they'll be questioned unfairly. Worse yet, they could be flagged as a troublemaker. Some people have a low tolerance for conflict. Others keep quiet because of a prior bad experience, or respond to internal negative running commentary that says, "How could you say something so stupid?"

Trust creates strong relationships that facilitate dialogue. Respect creates a smooth path toward dialogue. Competence facilitates the process. It's important to understand how to construct these elements so dialogue can flourish. You can master the third building block of dialogue by building, embracing, and evolving yourself and your team.

Build

We can't change human behavior by command, resolve, or good intentions. We can create a safe environment for people. When people feel safe, they are more aware of their thinking, their conversations, and their potential for better action. To build a safe place you must build trust, respect, and competence.

Build trust

Dialogue and relationships can't flourish without trust. You build trust by being trustworthy, trusting others, taking responsibility, and showing respect, consistency, and competency. Building trust starts with you. You risk personal loss when you trust another person. The idea of loss isn't very attractive, so you might demand proof of someone's trustworthiness before taking that risk. Here's the paradox: to develop trust you must take the risk without knowing how the other person will react.

You can facilitate the process of developing trust by taking small steps where the risk of loss is minimal. Then proceed from there. You can also create trust by helping others understand that people are emotional, not irrational. Controlled emotion is a normal, necessary, and expected component of dialogue. For all of these reasons, it takes time to build trust.

Trust is not built from the outside in, but from the inside out. It requires you to be clear about your personal values and beliefs, and to live by them. You need to understand your own behaviors and emotions. People trust leaders who demonstrate integrity. People are willing to support this kind of leader even in rocky spots and uncertain times.

You have to be trustworthy. When you promise something, deliver. When you say you won't punish people who share their thoughts and feelings, listen openly. When you say the space for dialogue is safe and you commit to a productive environment, don't let things get out of hand.

Excuses undermine trust

If you have been a leader for a while, you have probably heard all kinds of excuses for conversations gone wrong. People frequently excuse their own behavior by labeling others as abrasive, annoying, and insulting. Then they link those attributes to their own loss of control. What can you do? While you can't influence what others say or do, you can take responsibility for your own thoughts, actions, and reactions.

The way you talk to yourself makes a big difference in how you communicate and behave. For example, you can acknowledge that the recent merger brings uncertainty. But instead of thinking "no one has control of anything anymore," you can tell yourself that you can make a difference in how things are communicated.

When you take initiative and reach out to connect with the unknown, your words and behaviors convey your willingness to contribute to a safe process. This influences your ability to build trust.

Here are some suggestions for taking personal responsibility:

- Instead of shunning people or exchanging negative comments, ask questions that bring out the best in others.
- Instead of reacting negatively when someone says something annoying, use humor and ask the person to tell you a story about himself.
- Make positive comments about others.
- Rather than taking a comment personally, chalk it up to the person's communication style and offer up a compliment instead of an angry retort.

When you take responsibility for your thoughts, emotions, and the message you need to deliver, you will be able to speak with clarity, conviction, and compassion. How people feel after speaking with you will determine their interest in developing a relationship with you. It also affects the trust that develops. It will impact their trust in your ability to keep people engaged in safe dialogue. When relationships are on the line, there are no trivial comments.

People in dialogue develop trust together if they have boundaries to ensure a safe space. Here are four ground rules to establish a safe space:

1. *Don't accuse or attack.* People become defensive if they feel attacked. Encourage honesty about feelings and situations without resorting to cutting remarks. Trade "I" statements for "you" statements.
2. *Encourage honest exchanges.* The flow of accurate information encourages trust and creates a culture of openness.
3. *Listen with respect.* People won't share honest opinions if they feel disrespected. Listening with respect signals that you value people and their ideas.
4. *Ensure privacy.* This conversation is private. Period.

As you encourage team members to see their colleagues as people, trust will flow from within the group. Create situations that help them share personal stories, interests, and family reflections. It will help them bond. You might also encourage a lunch outing or happy hour where everyone can share a funny childhood story. The results can be lasting.

Much of this is possible and easy to achieve if the team works in the same geographic location. It can be trickier to build trust within a virtual team. You can facilitate trust building in a virtual team by thinking virtually. Here are some tips:

- Schedule a virtual meet-and-greet session.
- Create a blog where people can share their personal stories.
- Develop a graphic that illustrates the group's shared values, and those that are unique to individuals or cultures.
- Create a team charter that defines goals, roles, and protocols for sharing work digitally.
- Highlight individual areas of expertise and skills. Make sure everyone knows the value each individual contributes to the group.

- Encourage team members to be on time for conference calls or web meetings. They should also let the rest of the team know when they'll be absent, or on vacation.

While there are techniques for building trust virtually, team members should still make every effort to be on time for conference calls and meetings. Common courtesies still apply. In a virtual setting, keep your promises, as your word is often all you can give. You will set an example for others as you follow through on the promises you make from the leadership seat. Positive follow-through builds trust quickly, and can raise the entire group's tone and expectations.

Build respect

Imagine a world where:

- Everyone treats you with respect and dignity.
- You don't have to deal with gossips, liars, or bullies.
- Coworkers fix problems rather than place blame.
- You actually enjoy work, and you're productive.

If that sounds like the fantasy, there's good news. You can live in this fantasyland when you build your relationships on a foundation of trust and respect. To create respect, you must give respect. This is not accomplished by exhibiting bullying behaviors, like being overly demanding, critical and driven. Are you a glorified bully? Read and reflect:

- It's okay to criticize poor performance. But if you publicly criticize and humiliate, *you are being a bully.*
- It's okay to push people beyond their comfort zones. But if you force people to do things they're opposed to, *you are being a bully.*
- It's okay to have strong opinions and express them. But if you take feedback personally, become defensive, and ignore opinions, *you are being a bully.*
- It's okay to prefer working with certain people. But if you publicly favor or disfavor people, *you are being a bully.*

Notice the difference? A bully doesn't care about others. A bully is only interested in personal comfort and advancement, regardless of the damage. A respectful leader has a robust base of humility and shows respect and fairness. Successful leaders balance drive and determination with their respect for others. They use power appropriately. Here are some respectful behaviors worth mastering.

- Even when you are busy, pause and focus on people.
- Reprimand people in private. Address problems without belittling or threatening.
- Listen without interrupting mid-sentence.
- Take ideas and suggestions seriously.
- Stop to greet people with a smile, instead of passing them in frenzy.
- Expect the best of others without micro-managing the process

Incorporate these respectful behaviors in you daily life. Acknowledge these behaviors if you see them. Respect has become so scarce that many people forget what it looks like. They don't know how to practice it. As you practice respect, you will create loyalty, encourage more effective communication and foster innovation. Your workplace will regain its health, and you may see productivity and profits increase.

As you master respectful behavior, consider ways to bring more respect into your work environment. Here are four techniques:

1. *Teach it.* What is disrespectful behavior? Don't leave it open to subjective interpretations. Make your expectations of positive behavior clear and specific. Teach it. Respect is mandatory, not optional. Include it in annual reviews. Clearly defined boundaries build a culture of respect where everyone is accountable.

2. *Adapt it.* Frame ideas about respect within the context of your organization. While certain principles are universally accepted, such as treating others with respect, you will be well served to frame expectations around your company's unique culture. Be deliberate about your expectations. Have employees help draft the code of standards. With input, they will be more inclined to exceed your expectations.

3. *Model it.* It is your role as leader to personally step up and take responsibility for creating a culture of respect. Changing a culture of disrespect starts at the top. Model what you expect to see. Hold yourself accountable.

4. *Praise it.* Many people experience bullying in silence. They fear retaliation. Notice respectful behavior and praise it in public. What you praise you perpetuate. Lift up the positives of respect, honor, and civility. These strengths facilitate dialogue.

Sometimes people mistake respect with establishing a democratic workplace where everyone is treated with deference and politically correct politeness. Respect really means challenging each other to realize potential and solving problems together.

Build competence

Competence is a combination of knowledge, skills, and behaviors used to develop personally and professionally, and to perform well. Competency grows through experience and the extent to which people learn and adapt. Most people capitalize on their skills to improve performance. Today's successful professionals need to be competent in their technical and interpersonal skills. That's why building competence in dialogue is so important. Competent people help others become more competent. If you can build your own competence, you can help others build theirs. Consider these suggestions:

1. *Identify your strengths.* What kind of tasks do you learn quickly? Which communication skills come naturally? Ask yourself what gives you the greatest sense of satisfaction when participating in a dialogue.

2. *Set performance standards.* Commit to successfully complete specific goals to improve your dialogue skills. Clearly define your expectations. Establish a time period. Request feedback and use it to identify areas where your skills are lacking.

3. *Develop different communication styles.* You interact with others based on their relationship to you. Be flexible in how you build rapport with people. Modify your approach depending on the person and situation.

4. *Use critical thinking skills to decide a course of action.* When sharing your thoughts, support your reasoning with facts. Be open about approaches for problem solving. Don't just analyze a situation to get to the bottom of it. Make sure everyone in the dialogue analyzes, understands, and shares their thinking. Diversity of thought will result in better outcomes.

5. *Look for new opportunities.* What are you capable of accomplishing? Taking risks involves overcoming obstacles by using your strengths to the fullest advantage. Dream together. Find mentors. Welcome learning opportunities and seminars. The team's collective strengths will contribute to the quality of the dialogue.

6. *Anticipate potential setbacks.* This will help you handle unexpected situations. Talking as a team can help you analyze risks and resolve challenges, thereby improving performance.

7. *Practice social responsibility.* Being accountable can help boost your confidence. How willing are you to take risks that will benefit others? Consider your choices objectively, taking possible consequences into account. Encourage others to do the same. This will help create a corporate culture that is socially responsible and committed to dialogue.

A good way to foster competency development is to encourage people to find a mentor, take a class, attend a seminar, or engage in other learning activities that will enhance their skills as effective communicators.

Embrace

For dialogue to work well, you have to willingly embrace the mutuality of communication and the honesty it requires. As a result, you can joyfully embrace ideas and bring fun to the process. Positivity and appreciation smooth the path to dialogue.

Embrace mutuality

Mutuality is established as people listen and speak in search of understanding. Each regards the other as a partner in a shared inquiry, someone whose point of view is valued, someone with whom to explore the familiar and develop the new. In mutuality there is openness to influence, emotional availability, and a constantly changing rhythm of responding to and influencing the other's state

Mutuality, which is tied to trust building, acknowledges we are all inextricably tied together. At the heart of mutuality are openness and a willingness to constantly modify one's own understanding. Mutuality is the guiding attitude that makes the commitment and realization of understanding possible. It results in collaboration and profound connections. When you embrace mutuality, you believe the other person is unique, important, and worthy of your full attention.

True mutuality develops over time. It grows as your relationship deepens. A profound connection develops as you begin to know one another's heart and mind. As a leader, you know you cannot lead alone. Your individual study, research, reflection, and action are essential to your success. You must also be able to share your thoughts with others, and they must be willing to challenge your ideas. Here are the requirements for nurturing mutuality:

Time. To develop mutual relationships while providing encouragement through dialogue, you will have to spend old-fashioned face time with people. That time may come in the form of playing, working, planning, talking or arguing.

Vulnerability. Human relationships may cause some pain. Be willing to be uncomfortable and challenge each other while showing respect. Allow opportunities to forgive each other – and yourself – to evolve naturally.

Empathy. Mutual empathy is not a courtesy; it is a sophisticated skill that clears a critical pathway toward greater clarity, knowledge, and mutuality in relationships. It is a bridge where people from different perspectives can meet to engage in dialogue without overpowering, shaming, or humiliating each other. Mutual empathy allows people to authentically represent their experiences. This knowledge is essential for creating constructive dialogue.

Empowerment. Mutual empowerment grows out of mutual empathy. When people in a relationship feel seen, known, heard, and respected, they generate mutual empowerment. This dynamic process involves the feeling that everyone can impact the relationship and shape dialogue. Disempowering relationships make people feel drained, immobilized, confused, worthless, and isolated. These types of relationships discourage and obstruct dialogue. In contrast, mutually empowering relationships open the way to new growth opportunities.

Attitude. Attitude is everything. You must have the attitude that others' contributions are as valuable as yours. Continually remind yourself that you're interested in understanding other perspectives, and that you are prepared to lead and be led. It's also beneficial to remember that getting stuck is a shared problem.

When you embrace mutuality it's possible to take emotional and cognitive action that benefits everyone in the relationship. Even when there are functional hierarchies operating in relationships, like a pilot flying a plane or a CEO leading a company, mutuality facilitates the growth of everyone in the relationship. When scientists, artists, or leaders reexamine old theories that conflict with new insights, thinking together can be productive. That said, mutuality doesn't always come easily, and it's important to be aware of possible roadblocks:

Layering leads to hierarchical barriers that distort communication.

Centralization leads to gaps between decision makers and doers.

Power differences lead to status differentials.

No representation leads to monologues and lack of feedback from stakeholders.

Silos and conflict lead to blaming, lack of shared purpose and influence, and no one taking responsibility.

Judging self or others leads to positions of superiority or inferiority.

As a leader who assumes an attitude of equality, you will come to appreciate that your truth serves your team's truth and vice versa. Mutuality is nourished and sustained in effective working and living partnerships. When scientists, artists, or leaders reexamine old theories that conflict with new discoveries, they find thinking together particularly productive. Thinking and working collaboratively is especially promising in constructing new frameworks.

Embrace honesty

For dialogue to develop it's essential to embrace honesty. Honesty includes your words, as well as your authenticity and integrity. You must first be honest with yourself. Remove your mask, and then share your thoughts with integrity. It may seem natural, but many leaders have their reasons for not having honest conversations. Here are a few examples, followed by explanations of why they're ineffective:

> "*The truth is too scary for people to deal with it.*" This is often said in hard financial times or in the face of a dreaded merger. It's ineffective reasoning. People sense that something is wrong, and then non-truths circulate and do more damage than the authentic message.

> "*The less people know, the less they will worry.*" Wrong again. Accurate information helps ease unfounded worries. People find ways to deal with reality.

> "*If I admit that I don't know, people will lose respect for me.*" False. People respect leaders who admit their vulnerabilities. This also opens up possible collaboration to find a more creative solution.

Research suggests that organizations with leaders who engage others in honest communication perform in the top half – some in the top quartile – of their industry. It's a key statistic to consider as you evaluate the honesty of your conversations. Here are five areas you can focus on to further embrace honesty.

Be authentic   To be authentic, you must speak the truth and broadly present yourself in a genuine, bona fide way. It means you are worthy of acceptance and trustworthy, not a false imitation. Authenticity requires you to be true to yourself, colleagues, customers, friends and family. Being authentic calls for the courage to take risks, make mistakes, and learn from them. When you assume a constant position of learning, you will always be curious and ready for surprise.

Tell the truth   Don't tell others what they want to hear. Tell them the truth, even if they don't like the truth. In doing so, get beyond the official truth to reality. This is what people talk about around the water cooler. Address it. Though it may be tempting to ignore a difficult issue, speak to it with honesty.

To realize your vision, you must honestly face reality. To acquire knowledge, you must honestly admit what you don't know. To implement improvements, you must honestly analyze current data. You can only gain credibility and trust through honesty.

Be vulnerable   By beginning an honest conversation, you share your thoughts with honesty while also inviting feedback. There's a chance you won't like what you hear. That very feedback may lead to your future growth and success. Too many leaders have been trained in authority and certitude first, many times at the expense of transparency. Acknowledge what you don't know. Share your thoughts, and build connections.

Use tact   Honesty and tact go together. Honesty that lacks tact can become cruel. Tact without honesty leads to shallow, devious, and hypocritical interactions. Tact is using the appropriate words at the appropriate moment in an appropriate way. It requires patience and discipline to think before speaking. It requires choosing the right time to open the conversation. It demands kindness.

Develop a strong ethical conduct   Your values color your present and future actions. If you act dishonestly, you position yourself to blur future judgment. Withholding truth can be a disastrous business practice. If your ethical compass points to honesty, honest conversations will be your only path to dialogue.

Connections and bonds develop through mutual honest sharing. Truth, honesty, and openness serve as the connecting bonds in an organization. When you open your heart and lead through honest dialogue, people will follow you.

Embrace joy

Successful dialogue requires enjoyment not just in the end result, but also in the journey. It's important to enjoy interactions and moments of progress. Celebrate small advancements, just as parents do as their baby develops. As you lead the celebration, others will join in and share your joy. This practice spurs momentum and provides energy. It also provides a mind shift, from the tendency to measure progress by what's lacking to what is being accomplished.

For example, if dialogue used to break down an average of six times in a team meeting, and now it breaks down about three times, you could despair and believe you failed at dialogue. On the other hand, you could celebrate because you've improved by 100 percent. If you take the second approach, you will have more energy for your work and have joy for a job well done.

Words that build joy

Successful leaders understand the power of words. Catch yourself using words of joy. They're constructive and have a positive influence. Here are some examples:

> *Words of encouragement*: These are kind words that prop people up and make them feel good. They boost confidence and lead to increased efficiencies.

> *Words of affirmation*: Affirming words elevate and recognize others, which heal and foster positive relationships.

> *Words of direction*: Words create reality, which create culture. Use positive words to bring a positive reality to life.

Words can hurt and shock, or they can lift spirits and bring joy. Positive words are refreshing and uplifting. Some leaders think the only way to influence people is through threats and criticism. People respond out of fear. Other leaders use positive words and move people harmoniously toward exceptional results. What kind of power and influence do you want to wield? Positive influence is more desirable, leaves less collateral damage, and gets better results.

Will you embrace pain or joy?

Sometime in the 1500s, English poet Robert Herrick used the phrase "no pain, no gain" in his writings. He was conveying the idea that hard work results in positive benefits. Does the noble phrase from a well-respected poet still apply today? We grow so accustomed to thinking one way that we sometimes forget to challenge what we know, and then miss what's right in front of our eyes. Consider this example.

Mark was in a new and challenging leadership position. He wanted to be more effective and better positioned to improve his team's performance. After a few months of hard work, Mark's productivity was up, his clients were happy, deadlines were met, and conflicts had diminished considerably.

I was surprised when he expressed concern. He said, "Everyone on my team is so dedicated to the job and willing to cooperate, it almost feels like it's going too smoothly or that I make it too easy for people. What am I doing wrong?"

His uneasiness puzzled me, and then it hit me! Mark still believed work should be "painful." Regardless of the positive outcomes he was experiencing, he had the nagging feeling that people would think of him as a soft leader. He thought people would be less productive if they were stressed and fearful.

The same applies to dialogue. Many people think that unless a dialogue is filled with conflict and difficulties, it's not real, honest, or open. Evidence based on research and experience suggests that when people feel positive, calm, and collaborative, their dialogue is more productive. This kind of atmosphere also facilitates innovation, a competitive advantage.

Maybe it's time to abandon the "no pain, no gain" mentality and embrace a "no gain with pain" mindset. Leaders who can create a positive synergy will be in high demand and go far. Embrace joy! Even though an open dialogue does not entirely consist of positive words, embracing positive ways of talking yields better results. And doesn't embracing joy just feel better too?

Evolve

Finally, dialogue leads you to evolve. If you are not evolving, you and your organization are in decline. It is imperative to accept the reality of the present situation, make a feasible growth plan, and persevere until positive transformation brings liberation. Dialogue will transform the way you interact with others and take you to amazing places.

Accept reality

Things change. Stuff happens. Markets, economies, colleagues, customers, and you are in a constant state of change. Is it easier to ignore reality? Is it a simpler path? It may be, but ignorance will worsen the situation. Dialogue must be anchored in reality for it to go anywhere. Reality is never absolute. Your version of reality is as good as anyone's. You will gain clarity by considering all aspects of the topic in collaboration with others.

Interrogate reality

Question multiple realities. It will cause people to think. Ideas will emerge. Solutions will be the product of the group, not of one individual. People buy in to decisions when they feel their perspective was sought and valued, and when they understand why and how a decision was made.

Describe reality without placing blame

The more complex the problem, the stronger the urge to point fingers. This results in defensive behavior, which slams the door on dialogue and resolution. A very different conversation unfolds when all stakeholders describe the reality of the problem without laying blame. They share more information, gain deeper understanding, and arrive at thoughtful resolutions. Modify your language. Replace "but" with "and" and watch the conversation open.

Accept responsibility for your reality

Take ownership of your feelings, words, and actions. Have self control and pause before you speak. Learn to soothe yourself when the conversation stirs your emotions. If you see others struggling with their feelings, call time out so everyone can regroup.

Also resist the urge to blame others for your failure to communicate. If you accept responsibility, you can change the result. Your behavior is the only thing under your control. Changing the result is as simple, or as hard, as changing your behavior.

Accept influence

When leaders have trouble accepting influence, or influencing others, arguments can result. No one wants to admit being wrong. The reasonable alternative is to accept influence. If you want to influence others and deal with conflict, you must first be willing to be influenced.

Aikido, a Japanese martial art, teaches, "Yield to win." It is based on non-collision and non-resistance with opposing forces so anyone can employ it with the least amount of physical strength. What do you do when someone pushes you? In the Western world people push back. If you push back you can win, lose, or end in a stalemate, none of which is conducive to mutual satisfaction.

In Aikido, you move toward the attacker and slightly off the line of attack, simultaneously making a turn that leaves you next to the attacker and facing in the same direction. From this position you look at the situation from the attacker's viewpoint while maintaining your own. It immediately multiplies your options.

Instead of meeting a verbal attack with a verbal counterattack, respond by coming around to the other's viewpoint by entering into it and blending with it. This is very disarming. It will change the energy of the conversation and allow you to approach the conflict from the same perspective. It will build understanding. You can ask questions such as:

- Can you please explain your thinking?

- What are your feelings on this issue?
- Can you tell me why this is so important to you?

This will help increase the possibility of understanding the other person's reality while influencing thinking. It will help you discover ways to meet the needs of all parties.

Accept diversity

Good dialogue avoids think tank mentality. The multiplicity and diversity of thought enriches dialogue and leads to stronger conclusions. Accept, value, and celebrate all people with their uniqueness and ideas. Make them feel essential to the organization's success. Using the diversity already present in your organization is a brilliant way to gain competitive advantage. If your leadership team is grappling with an issue, why not invite diverse people from all fields and levels to brainstorm? Their contributions could surprise you and make a profound impact.

Here are some questions to ponder: How diverse is your own thinking and that of your closest associates? How good are you at accepting others' unique ways of thinking? Are you excited about the varied personalities and individual preferences that surround you? Can you appreciate differences, or do you view them primarily as a source of friction and annoyance? What can you do to encourage a dialogue that is more diversity friendly?

If you implement ways to capitalize on diverse ideas, a synergy will move your dialogues and organization forward.

Grow together

Employee engagement drives the bottom line. You have the power to nourish motivation. But how? The answer is so simple that very few leaders recognize it. Teresa Amabile, Edsel Bryant Ford Professor of Business Administration and Director of Research at Harvard Business School, studies how everyday life in organizations influences people and their performance. Her answer is the Progress Principle. It suggests that the single most important thing managers can do to engage employees is celebrate the small win – incremental progress toward a meaningful goal. In other words: if you talk together, you grow and perform well together.

There are four phases of dialogue for growth. Over time, people move through the four phases several times and in many ways. It's important for leaders and employees to look back and note career development linked to dialogue. They should measure how dialogue has helped foster understanding and improve conflict management skills.

1. *Reflect.* Reflective conversations allow people to discuss motivations, search for awareness of intentions and desires, and outline understanding of key points. Reflection leads to growth.

2. *Envision.* After reflecting on the past and present, resist the temptation to jump to an immediate decision. Instead, encourage stakeholders to determine a vision. This gives the dialogue direction and movement.

3. *Explore*: People tend to begin their dialogues at this step, wanting to immediately explore problems and solutions. Rather than jump in here, it's critical to understand the past, envision, the future and then explore options. This approach helps paint the full picture.

4. *Act*: The goal of dialogue for growth is learning and change. Each person's path to change is unique. Motivating people to act can be difficult. Some people get stuck in the option cycle. Trivial details sidetrack others. Help individuals determine the appropriate sequence for actions and tasks. Offer insight on how to measure success.

To take action successfully:

Set clear goals. This should be done in dialogue. When people know where their work is heading and why it matters (the big picture), goals provide mileposts to measure progress. People become frustrated and lose motivation if there are conflicting priorities or unclear, meaningless, and arbitrary goals. Weak goals waste time and stunt growth. People gain motivation to take action when they have clear and specific goals, and when you hold them accountable. Small daily wins provide the momentum for ongoing growth.

Practice connected autonomy. Once decisions are made together, people need to feel confident that they can take action without further approval. It's important for your team members to feel capable, creative, and that they have a say in their work. They need to know you support their daily decisions.

Learn from problems and successes. Face problems head on to facilitate growth and learning. Analyze them. Make plans to overcome them or learn from them. Learning from successes is also important. It's common to have a wrap-up dialogue after successfully completing a project. It's also common to scrutinize what you can learn from mistakes. But what would happen if you analyzed what you could learn from the success? You might realize that the group developed several creative solutions that could be used in the future. If you don't discuss successes, you risk losing quality creativity and growth opportunities for the team.

Encourage and allow ideas to flow. Some of the best action and growth happens when ideas about projects flow freely within the team and across the organization. Silo mentality stunts growth. Ideas flow best when leaders truly listen to their workers, encourage vigorous dialogue of diverse perspectives, and respect constructive criticism.

Provide interpersonal support. People feel more connected to others and ready to grow when their emotions are validated. At times, dialogue can be frustrating, sad, or exhilarating. Acknowledging people's frustrations and joys can alleviate negative emotions and amplify the positive. When someone shares emotions in dialogue, empathetic ears and words can go a long way in easing minds and allowing dialogue to flow. People can nourish and support each other's growth. For support to happen, create opportunities for friendships to develop and promote camaraderie. As a leader, you are most effective when you serve the needs of people as human beings.

Make time for reflection in action. As you take action, you must constantly reflect for learning and growth to occur. Take time daily to convene your team. Ask about progress, question challenges, and gauge the need to revise goals for the growth of all. Don't wait for a problem to become a crisis before discussing it. If you reflect as you act, you can learn and tweak your actions as needed.

Nothing encourages growth more than a nonjudgmental openness to listening and willingness to discuss anything that arises from dialogue.

Transform into the future

All human groups, including organizations and corporations, are living systems. They are as adaptive and unpredictable as the people who comprise them. Living systems change and transform. Consider these factors when you're framing the concept of the organization as a living system.

Participation

Everyone in a group influences and reflects the thinking and interaction of the whole. Powerful patterns of influence resonate throughout the organization, not just up and down the hierarchy. For this reason, it's important to include all voices in a dialogue. People want to share their perspective. Fulfill their desire and comprehend their input.

Context

Living systems evolve to meet environmental challenges and constraints. Thus, in organizations, there is always a reason why a situation evolves as it does. Strive to gain a clear-sighted understanding of why and how things function as they do. This sets the stage to work in reality rather than through illusions.

Unfolding Potential

Just like living systems grow and mature, so do living organizations. Apply this principle to discern what's possible now given the current reality, and what the future might hold. As you come together in dialogue it's easier to envision the future potential of the group.

Awareness

Living systems are characterized by an awareness of self and the environment. A system's ability to be aware of its actions as they unfold is a sophisticated change avenue. The most effective way for you to intervene is to increase the system's capacity to detect and correct errors, and identify and use strengths. A system's ability to reflect influences its capacity to take action.

When you design and promote generative conversations that foster awareness and capability, you facilitate transformation. Dialogue is the perfect catalyst for transformation.

9 Final Thoughts: Be ready for transformational change

L EADERS OFTEN SENSE change is needed; however, they're confused about what kind of change. Their change efforts fail because they try to implement incremental change, or make changes to behaviors and operations. What they really need is transformational change.

Transformational change is necessary when ideas originally designed to create order and stability no longer work. Frames of reference, thinking, and behavior need a fundamental shift. It takes a bold, compelling force to create that change. Transformational change breaks former molds and distorts existing patterns of action.

Transformative change is profound, fundamental, and irreversible. It's a metamorphosis. It starts with a hefty dose of fearlessness and innovation, and ends with a completely different organization. Robert Gass, co-founder of the Rockwood Leadership Institute, best explains the elements of transformational change. Here's a summary of key points:

1. *Transformational change is holistic.* It's a systems approach that attends equally to hearts and minds, behavior and social structures. It aims to be irreversible and enduring. It calls for everyone to engage in dialogue.

2. *Transformation focuses on acting in the present.* While honoring the lessons of the past and planning for the future, transformation has a strong focus on what's happening right now. The process of transformational change must mirror what it seeks to create.

3. *Transformational change accentuates the positive.* It taps the power of a positive vision while identifying and addressing what's in need of change. By focusing on what's possible, energy and hope create

focus. It blends critique with an appreciation for what is already good and useful.

4. *Transformational change balances control with letting go.* The process of transformational change underscores the notion that the only constant is change. Instead of attempting to dominate life, you keep a dance of dynamic interaction with what happens around you. Transformational change values dynamic interaction and a humble approach to reality. The art of transformation lies in giving attention to what is, while skillfully working in harmony with what is alive and evolving in the world.

5. *Transformational change relies on communication and collaboration.* Because of its interdisciplinary nature, transformational change requires a high level of commitment and skill in open communication. It calls for working in partnerships and engaging with client needs, social trends, and unseen forces. All of this requires open dialogue.

6. *Transformational change engages the heart.* Many leaders try to engage people through facts and analysis. Intellect has its role, but transformational change requires a heartfelt approach to leadership. Transformational change activates collective action, and also helps break down walls that alienate people. Sharing stories from the heart moves people to engage in dialogue.

7. *Transformational change must happen at every level.* This kind of change is not individualistic or departmental. It requires the effort of every rank. Sometimes people in the least glamorous positions have the best understanding of what needs to happen and why. All voices are required to transform a performance into a work of art.

As you come to this book's end and reflect on transformative conversations in your own leadership journey, I leave you with this final thought.

Alan Deutschman, in his remarkably insightful book *Change or Die: The Three Keys to Change at Work and in Life*, offers research into change-or-die scenarios. His work focuses on patients facing bypass surgery and diseases that they can overcome with lifestyle changes. When faced with the reality that they must change or die, 90 percent do not alter their behavior. They choose death over transformation.

People in business are not much different.

I urge you to be among the 10 percent who chose transformation. These lasting lessons will help guide your transformation.

- Find fellowship that inspires you.
- Reframe disaster as possibility.
- Redefine assumptions that guide your behavior.
- Use disturbance in your life as a chance to redefine your future.
- Experiment and learn from your successes and failures.
- Design a process and cultivate a rich environment that supports openness.
- Most importantly, don't do it alone.

As a leader, shift from operating in a fortress to embracing new ideas, products, services, and solutions. This requires the courage and foresight to transform. Transformative change involves emergence, discovery, and invention. For it to work you must engage in collective dialogues and make meaning as a unified body. Change can be disruptive. Even terrifying. But it can also be exhilarating and bring the fresh energy needed for innovation. Allow dialogue to guide you through powerful transformations on your ever-changing leadership journey.

Acknowledgements

Thank you to the many executive coaches, research participants, and the following individuals and organizations for informing and inspiring my leadership journey. Your valuable wisdom contributed to my transformative learning and the creation of this book.

B. Akande; T. Andersen; H. Anderson; B. J. Avolio; L. Beca; M. Blalock; P. Block; D. Bohm; B. Brown; M. Buber; W.W. Burke; M.C. Clark; K. Cameron; D. Cooperrider; L. Cozolino; A. Deutschman; K. Domenici; P. Freire; H. Gardner; R. Gass; B. George; S. Godin; H. Goolishian; J. Habermas; R. Herrick; R.L. Howe; W. Isaacs; D. Kantor; R. Kent; R.R. Kilburg; J. Kotter; W. Lehr; S. Littlejohn; G. H. Litwin; F Luthans; J. Magruder; V.J. Marsick; H. Maturana; X May; C.L. Rassieur; D. Rock; P. Senge; J. Shotter; S. Srivastva; E.W. Taylor; A. Trosten-Bloom; L Vygotsky; F. Walumba; M. Wheatley; D. Whitney; D. Whyte; D. Yankelovich; L. Yorks; American Management Association; Center for Creative Leadership; HeartMath; Rockwood Leadership Institute; Siemens Enterprise Communications; SIS International Research; Watson Wyatt.

About the Author

Dr. Ada Gonzalez is an executive coach, facilitator, and a consultant in organizational development. She works with leaders, businesses and organizations to facilitate change, development and growth through dialogue. She shows business leaders how to discover the power of leading through conversations.

For more than 25 years as a change agent, and crafter of organizational dialogue, Gonzalez has provided support and created a safe space for development, learning, and growth.

More specifically, she translates theory and research findings into practice in day-to-day activities, supporting business strategy and results. Those who work with her have found a reduction in conflict and optimization of time and energy. Managers and organizations achieve increased collaboration and quick adaptation to challenges with the result being increased innovation and profitable growth.

Gonzalez and her consulting practice are grounded on research and experience. The principles of dialogue, organizational transformative learning, collaboration, and systems change are employed to reach growth goals.

She serves as an adjunct professor for the University of Delaware. In addition to undergraduate and graduate work at Andrews University in Michigan, she earned her Ph.D. at the Union Institute and University on Organizational Behavior, with an emphasis on leadership, dialogue, and change.

Dr. Ada has lived in several countries and her multicultural experiences and fluency in both Spanish and English have contributed to shaping who she is, as well as how she communicates and interacts with the world. She also has a multidisciplinary education and approach to leadership and communication. As an experienced and effective presenter she has designed and delivered courses, seminars, and workshops in the United States, as well as in many Latin American and several European countries.

Her specialties include leadership development, executive coaching, organizational cultural change, conflict resolution, assessment, dialogue and collaboration. She helps individuals and organizations understand, manage, and effectively promote change for gaining a competitive advantage. The achieved growth and transformation will help leaders acquire the new skills, mindset, and vision required for surviving and thriving into the future.

In her free time Dr. Ada enjoys traveling, playing the piano, and having open conversations with her husband Roger, her sons, and her friends.

To learn more about Dr. Ada's seminars, speaking, and programs, visit
her Web site:
http://logosnoesis.com
For more information, call 302-399-3915
e-mail address:
ada@logosnoesis.com

Special Offer: Say Goodbye to Unproductive Meetings!

Have you ever attended a meeting that went on and on—and nothing was accomplished? Were people bored, sleepy, or doing their own thing? Did the speaker drone on and on? If so, you're probably wondering, what's the secret to productive and lively meetings?
In this free special report you will discover:

- The big secret for better meetings

- How to craft a productive meeting

- How to start in a way that encourages collaboration

- How to welcome open dialogue

Get the free special report "Say Goodbye to Unproductive Meetings!" here:
http://logosnoesis.com/unproductive-meetings-offer

www.ingramcontent.com/pod-product-compliance
Lightning Source LLC
Chambersburg PA
CBHW060558200326
41521CB00007B/608